HARDING'S ELECTION AND ADMINISTRATION

SENATOR HARDING made a dignified campaign, following the example set by Governor McKinley in 1896. He did not leave his front porch in Marion, but received delegations that called on him, and made speeches which were sent broadcast. His plurality of 7,000,000 in November, 1920, was the largest ever received by any candidate, on any ticket, for any office.

December 26, 1920, I wrote the President-elect that the newspapers reported he had applications for every office in his gift, and wondered if he had given the office of "brutal friend" to any one. If not, I made application, as it was the office I had held under McKinley, Roosevelt, Taft, and Wilson.

He wrote me the following letter, which he has given me permission to publish:

UNITED STATES SENATE

WASHINGTON, D. C.

Marion, Ohio, January 2, 1921.

MR. H. H. KOHLSAAT,
  c/o The Biltmore Hotel,
    New York City, N. Y.

My dear Mr. Kohlsaat:

It was a joy to have such a letter as you wrote under date of December 26th, and I will be very glad to have

tration in Washington to straighten out the aftermath of the World War. Friday, June 11, he led the voting with the largest number of delegates, but was defeated by the unfortunate blunder of sending $2,500 to each of two men in Missouri, who put the money into their own pockets, going to the convention themselves as delegates. The money was sent to them for hall rent, music, and other legitimate expenses; as honorable men they should have returned the money as unspent.

The incident was seized upon by Hiram Johnson and his friends as an attempt to buy the Presidency. It was a false issue. They knew it, but it accomplished its purpose.

Saturday afternoon, the 12th, Senator Harding was nominated, Governor Lowden throwing his delegates and influence to him. At night Governor Coolidge, of Massachusetts, was nominated for the Vice-Presidency, the nomination he would probably have received if Governor Lowden had been successful and had control of the Vice-Presidency nomination.

FROM
McKINLEY TO HARDING

PRESIDENT McKINLEY

FROM
McKINLEY TO HARDING

PERSONAL RECOLLECTIONS OF
OUR PRESIDENTS

BY

H. H. KOHLSAAT

ILLUSTRATED

CHARLES SCRIBNER'S SONS
NEW YORK · LONDON
1923

TO MY WIFE

THROUGH the courtesy of the Curtis Publishing Company I am issuing in book form this series of articles, which first appeared in the columns of *The Saturday Evening Post*, with some chapters that did not appear in that magazine.

To Mr. George Horace Lorimer, editor, I wish to acknowledge a deep sense of appreciation for the encouragement he gave me in the writing of my "Personal Recollections of Our Presidents."

H. H. KOHLSAAT.

CONTENTS

CONTENTS

ILLUSTRATIONS

I

MY FIRST MEETING WITH McKINLEY

THE first time I met Major William McKinley was in Canton the day after the Presidential election of 1876. Gus Dannemiller introduced me to him with the remark: "Let me introduce you to our next congressman. This is Major McKinley's first term; he will be heard from."

McKinley was an extremely handsome young fellow of thirty-three, with an air of distinction that drew me to him at once. I was ten years his junior and believed Mr. Dannemiller was right when he said: "He will be heard from."

We seldom met until I was an alternate in the Republican national convention of 1888 in Chicago.

McKinley was chairman of the Ohio delegation. When the nominations for President were made, McKinley in an eloquent speech nominated John Sherman, of Ohio. During the balloting some one cast a vote for McKinley. It received great applause from the convention. When the cheering subsided, McKinley mounted a chair. His face was white and tense. In a voice full of emotion he said:

Mr. President and Gentlemen of the Convention:

I am here as one of the chosen representatives of my State. I am here by resolution of the Republican State

1

convention, passed without a single dissenting voice, commanding me to cast my vote for John Sherman for President, and to use every worthy endeavor for his nomination. I accepted the trust because my heart and judgment are in accord with the letter and spirit and purpose of that resolution. It has pleased certain delegates to cast their votes for me for President. I am not insensible of the honor they would do me, but in the presence of the duty resting upon me, I cannot remain silent with honor. I cannot, consistently with the wish of the State whose credentials I bear, and which has trusted me; I cannot with fidelity to John Sherman, who has trusted me in his cause and with his confidence; I cannot, consistently with my own views of personal integrity, consent or seem to consent, to permit my name to be used as a candidate before this convention. I should not respect myself if I could find it in my heart to do so, or permit to be done that which could even be ground for any one to suspect that I wavered in my loyalty to Ohio, or my devotion to the chief of her choice and the chief of mine. I do not request—I demand, that no delegates who would not cast reflection upon me shall cast a ballot for me.

The effect on the convention was dramatic. For a moment there was dead silence; then they broke into cheers and McKinley was more than ever the popular favorite.

The Illinois delegation was instructed for Judge Walter Q. Gresham.

As the fight developed against John Sherman, Indiana put Senator Benjamin Harrison in nomination. Mr. Harrison, who was in Chicago when his name was proposed, left for Indianapolis, his home. He was finally nominated, and was elected in November. In the years from 1889 to 1891 I saw McKinley frequently, and when I purchased the control of *The Inter-Ocean* in 1891, we came in contact very often. I never lost my youthful ambition to see him President.

II

THE REPUBLICAN NATIONAL CONVENTION
OF 1892

In 1892 the Republican organization offered me a place on the Illinois delegation to the national convention in Minneapolis. I accepted with the understanding that after the first ballot, for the renomination of President Harrison, I was free to vote for whom I pleased. Only one vote was taken, however, and Mr. Harrison was renominated.

My vote was for Harrison. My choice was McKinley. I did not like President Harrison. Although I recognized his ability and honesty, his manner chilled me. Many people admired him, but he had very few warm friends. It was said of him by Tom Reed that "Senator Harrison carried his lunch in his coat-tail pocket during the Senate session and then ate a cold lunch."

I came in personal touch with him two or three times, but there was no contact of enthusiasm. Perhaps I was somewhat prejudiced by our Illinois senator, Charles B. Farwell, who hated Harrison with all his nature.

There was little in common between the two men —both Presbyterians, but of different schools. Senator Farwell was famed as a poker-player and "sat in" many a game with Marshall Field, George M. Pullman, and John W. Doane.

It is told of Mr. Farwell that his wife, a devoutly Christian woman, remonstrated with him at one time, saying: "Charlie, I wish you would stop playing poker. It has a bad effect on the children." He answered: "Why, mother, don't you worry; we only play for a five-cent limit!" "I know," she answered, "but why have any limit?"

President Harrison and Senator Farwell fell out over patronage. It was said of Mr. Harrison that when he gave a man an office he did it in such a churlish way that the recipient went away angry. McKinley's manner was in great contrast with his. Senator "Billy" Mason used to say that when McKinley could not give a man an office he looked so unhappy about it the seeker would go away filled with sympathy for the President.

I was present once when a labor leader asked McKinley for some favor he could not grant. The man was hurt and rather truculent. McKinley told him how pained he was to refuse his request, and as he shook hands with him asked him if he was married. Taking a carnation from his coat he gave it to him, saying: "Give this to your wife with my compliments and best wishes." The astonished man smiled and said: "I would rather have this flower from you for my wife than the thing I came to get."

McKinley made a lifelong friend of that man and of his wife.

During the pre-convention days of 1892 Eugene Field, in his "Sharps and Flats" column of the Chicago *Daily News*, printed an item to the effect that I was going to Minneapolis to work for the nomination of a colored man on the ticket for Vice-President, and that I would pay the expenses of any colored man who would go to Minneapolis to help secure the nomination for one of his race. Field knew of my interest in bettering the condition of the colored people in Chicago through library and reading-rooms, and played on that fact.

The next morning when I arrived at my office in the Inter-Ocean Building the halls were filled with colored men and women eager for the trip. It took a good deal of explaining to convince them that it was one of Field's jokes! Some of the small Southern newspapers took it seriously, and I was subjected to a lot of comment more forcible than elegant.

William E. Curtis, of whom Field had borrowed $150 some years before, came to Chicago from Washington en route to the Minneapolis convention. He called on Field and reminded him of his debt.

Next day Field printed this paragraph in his column:

William E. Curtis, the well-known correspondent of the Chicago *Record*, is in the city for a few days looking after some of his permanent investments!

There are few places in the country hotter than Minneapolis after the middle of June, and the June of 1892 was no exception. The convention was held in a newly erected building, finished on the inside with fresh, unseasoned pine, from which the rosin dripped continually under the awful heat from the sun and the 15,000 or so human beings crowded under its roof.

My seat in the Illinois delegation was directly in front, close to the platform. McKinley was chairman of the convention. When the balloting began he was fanning himself gently with a large palm-leaf. Without any warning somebody started voting for him for President. He looked down at me and shook his head and began to move his fan faster and faster. As the voting proceeded he became very much agitated, and when Ohio cast her vote for him he challenged it, as his proxy had voted for him. But President Harrison won, although it is doubtful if he could have done so on a second ballot. Blaine and McKinley polled within one-half of a vote of each other.

During the nomination for Vice-President a delegate from Tennessee, with a delicious Southern accent, got up and said: "I nominate for Vice-President that grand old man from Maine, Thomas B. Reed."

One of the Maine delegates asked him by what

right he proposed Mr. Reed, as he was not a candidate. The Tennessee man came back with: "By no right, suh. I do not know the gentleman. I wouldn't know him if I met him in the middle of the road, suh, but no man is too big, suh, to be Vice-President of the United States, suh!"

Whitelaw Reid was put in nomination, and during the speeches Chauncey M. Depew came to me and asked what effect Mr. Reid's fight with "Big Six" of the Typographical Union would have. I told him I didn't know. Mr. Reid received the nomination.

After the convention adjourned I left the hall and went to the West Hotel. As I arrived at the hotel entrance an enthusiastic crowd surrounded McKinley's carriage and took him on their shoulders and carried him into the hotel. McKinley looked very distressed and unhappy, and more so when he saw that the leg of his trousers was up nearly to his knee, exposing his bare skin and his garter. He vainly tried to pull it down, but feared losing his balance.

They finally dropped him at the elevator and he asked me to take him to my room, as he knew he would find his room crowded. He was exhausted with the heat and excitement. On entering my room he at once removed his outer clothing and, clad only in his underwear, lay down on the bed, from which I had thrown back all the covering. I did the same. Nothing was said by either of us until a knock came at the door and some one from Mark Hanna asked if McKinley was in the room. I said: "Yes, but Major McKinley does not want it known, as he is 'all in.'" McKinley said: "Tell Mark to come up here." When Hanna arrived I took the top sheet and threw it over one of those awful plush sofas. Hanna stripped to his underwear, and all three of us lay panting for breath. Some ice-water revived us. Hardly a word was spoken for fifteen minutes or so. Finally Mr. Hanna said: "My God, William, that was a damned close squeak!"

There was no real intention of nominating McKinley in 1892, as it was felt no Republican could be elected—it was not a Republican year; but I am sure that Mr. Hanna thought if McKinley made a good showing in the convention of 1892 it might help him to win in 1896. The first work for McKinley's nomination was done in that room by three men in their underclothes.

III

GOVERNOR McKINLEY'S DEBTS

Mr. Hanna's fear that 1892 was not a Republican year was realized. President Harrison was defeated, and Grover Cleveland elected for the second time.

But the organization to nominate McKinley in 1896 was actively at work. The most minute detail was not neglected. Each man who declared himself favorable to McKinley's nomination was enrolled alphabetically under Mr. Hanna's supervision.

McKinley was governor of Ohio, and in constant touch with the situation through visits to Mr. Hanna and Myron T. Herrick in Cleveland, and through both of them on their visits to Columbus.

February, 1893, Governor McKinley promised to deliver the Washington's Birthday address before the Ohio Society of New York.

I was in New York at the time, stopping at the Holland House. Eugene Field had come with me as my guest for a few days' rest. We were eating breakfast Saturday, the 22d, when Field exclaimed, "Good Lord! McKinley is busted!" and read me a despatch from Newcastle, Pa., saying McKinley had received word that a friend of his, Robert L.

10

Walker, of Youngstown, had failed, and that he had turned back to Youngstown and wired New York cancelling his engagement with the Ohio Society.

The despatch stated that Governor McKinley was on Walker's notes to the extent of $17,000.

I knew something of McKinley's finances and did not believe he could raise $17,000 cash. So I left Field at the breakfast-table and wired the governor at Youngstown: "Have just read of your misfortune. My purse is open to you. Am going to Chicago to-night. Will meet you anywhere you say in Ohio." Later in the day I received a telegram from him saying: "Take the 6 o'clock train. Will meet you at the depot in Cleveland Sunday morning."

I learned later that Mr. Walker had advanced McKinley $2,000 every two years in a number of his campaigns to pay his assessments. McKinley repaid him $1,000 a year out of his salary as congressman, which at that time was $5,000 a year. He lived at the old Ebbitt House in Washington with his wife, in a couple of small rooms.

In 1892 Mr. Walker asked McKinley if he could help him to tide over for a short time. He was a manufacturer and was suffering from the general depression which led up to the panic of 1893.

McKinley said: "I will give you everything I have. You have been my friend through so many campaigns. I own about $17,000 worth of stock in different industrial enterprises in my district." Walker answered: "I am afraid the banks will not loan on your collateral, but if you will indorse my notes for that amount I can get the money." McKinley agreed to indorse to the amount of $17,000, believing he could make good if necessary.

To return to February, 1893. The Sunday-morning Buffalo papers announced that instead of being on Walker's notes for $17,000, the amount at midnight had arisen to $98,000.

On arriving in Cleveland about 9 o'clock Sunday morning, McKinley and Myron T. Herrick met me as I stepped out of the car. McKinley was pale and wan, with black rings under his eyes. He put his hand on my shoulder, but could not speak for his emotion. Tears rolled down his cheeks. We went directly to the Herrick home. On our way the governor was much depressed. I asked him how much he was in debt. He said: "I don't know—it may be $100,000, $200,000, or $500,000."

It seems that when the notes came due, Walker would write McKinley at Columbus that a note for $2,000 or so in such and such a bank would come due on a certain date, and he did not know whether the bank would renew in full or demand a reduction. That if McKinley would sign it in blank he would fill in the amount. With his sublime faith in his friend, McKinley did so. Then Walker raised shoulder and said: "I have wanted to say something to you for over three years. When you put that item in the papers in February, '93, that I would pay my debts in full and closed the mouths of my critics, you did me a great service. I owe more to you than any one in the world, except my mother, for I should probably have gone to the penitentiary instead of the White House!"

I told him he was wrong, as he had never done a dishonest thing in his life, and that Walker would be in the penitentiary if he had prosecuted him instead of forgiving him for the great wrong he did.

To return to the meeting with Mr. Hanna in my office, Monday morning, February 24, 1893, I told him of my suggestion that trustees be appointed to receive the McKinley properties. He fully agreed with me that it was the course to pursue. We drew up an agreement to pay a certain sum to liquidate McKinley's debts and signed our names. I have the paper now. It shows over $40,000 raised in Chicago. Mr. Hanna and Mr. Herrick secured a generous sum in Cleveland. Mr. Hanna wired me to meet him in Pittsburgh. We went to the Duquesne Club and met Philander C. Knox and some of his and Mr. Hanna's friends. When we left the club we had, as I remember now, $120,000 total subscriptions. Mr. Hanna went on to Philadelphia and completed the $130,000 needed. New York was not asked for a cent.   There were over 5,000 subscribers to the fund.

Mr. Herrick called upon the banks in Ohio holding the Walker-McKinley paper and asked them to contribute 10 per cent of the amount of notes which they held, which they agreed to do, and he repaid them in full.

With the $13,000 left over, Mr. Herrick paid a mortgage of $10,000 due on the McKinley Opera House in Canton, and deposited $3,000 in bank to meet current and subsequent bills.

Previous to securing the subscriptions three trustees—Judge William R. Day, Myron T. Herrick, and H. H. Kohlsaat—were appointed. To them Governor and Mrs. McKinley turned over all their property.

Judge Day, who handled the matter in Canton—now an ex-justice of the Supreme Court—told me that not one single claim was filed against the estate.

Governor McKinley never knew who contributed the money. The list of subscribers was refused him later when he asked for it, declaring he would pay them back with the money he saved out of his salary as President, and turned over as he received it to Mr. Herrick, who made some fortunate investments, which gave McKinley's estate some $200,000. The governor's appreciation of our efforts was expressed in the following letter:

Columbus Feb 26/93

Dear Mr Kohlsaat:

The pen will not — can not
speak what is in my heart this morning, Your letter
is so full of personal sweetness — the expressions of
Chicago friends, whom you quote, are so tender and
generous, that my heart overflows with thanksgiving.
Did ever man and wife have such friends and
how can we ever repay them?
My mail is larger than ever before in my life and so
bounding with kindness and sympathy and offers of material
aid; I am standing up with courage, yet the support
of my friends & their confidence in my integrity moves me
deeply, I wish you might see my letters and telegrams,
Your thoughtful suggestion about my immediate needs is
gratefully noted, but with my salary which in a few days will
be paid to me. I will be able to get along comfortably.
Give to my Chicago friends the warm and lasting gratitude
of Mrs McKinley & myself. God bless you my unselfish friend and
give to your home & household his tender care
Your sincere friend
Wm McKinley Jr

Mr H H Kohlsaat,
Chicago Ill

STATE OF OHIO

EXECUTIVE DEPARTMENT

OFFICE OF THE GOVERNOR

Columbus Feb. 26, 1893.

DEAR MR. KOHLSAAT:

The pen will not—can not speak what is in my heart this morning, your letter is so full of personal sweetness—expressions of Chicago friends whom you quote are so tender and generous that my heart overflows with thanksgiving.

Did ever man and wife have such friends and how can we ever repay them?

My mail is larger than ever before in my life and so abounding with kindness and sympathy and offers of material aid. I am standing up with courage. Yet, the support of my friends and their confidence in my integrity moves me deeply. I wish you might see my letters and telegrams.

Your thoughtful suggestion about my immediate wants is gratefully noted but, with my salary which in a few days will be paid to me, I will be able to get along comfortably.

Give to my Chicago friends the warm and lasting gratitude of Mrs. McKinley and myself. God bless you, my unselfish friend, and give to your home and household His tender care.

Your sincere friend,

WILLIAM McKINLEY, JR.

Mr. H. H. Kohlsaat,
Chicago, Ill.

IV

McKINLEY AND THE A. P. A. IN 1893

On Saturday in the early fall of '93, Governor Mc-
Kinley telephoned from Columbus, asking my wife
and me to spend Sunday with him and Mrs. McKinley in that city. He met us at the station and took
us to the Neil House, where he lived while governor
of Ohio.

After luncheon he and I went into his bedroom
and he told me that he had received a call Friday
from a committee of the A. P. A. (an anti-Catholic
organization) demanding the discharge of two guards
in the Ohio Penitentiary, on no other grounds than
that they were Catholics. "This is a test case,"
they said. "We will call Monday morning at 10
o'clock for your answer."

The governor said he argued with them about
religious liberty, etc., but they were unyielding and
left, promising to return for his answer.

McKinley was candidate for re-election for governor in November. He had won in 1891 by a plurality of 21,511. There were 63,000 A. P. A.'s in
Ohio and 90 per cent of them Republicans. It
seemed almost certain defeat to lose their votes.
After stating the situation he said: "What would you

say to them?" "I would tell them to go to h——l," I replied.

McKinley, a devout Methodist, said: "I shall not say that, but I will tell them that under our Constitution a man is guaranteed his religious liberty, and until these men do something that will warrant their discharge, they will hold their places."

A few days later Governor McKinley told Mr. Hanna of the A. P. A. demand, and his answer. It didn't take wise old Mark Hanna long to act. Without telling McKinley his plans, he went to Cincinnati and wired Captain E. J. Vattmann, Catholic chaplain, stationed at Fort Thomas, Ky., to come to Cincinnati. Father Vattmann was appointed by President Harrison at the request of McKinley, when he was in Congress. Vattmann loved Governor McKinley, and when told of the A. P. A. threat he said: "Leave it to me."

A few days later Bishop Elder, of Cincinnati, and Bishop Horstmann, in Cleveland, gave interviews commending McKinley for his wise administration of public institutions in Ohio, and expressed the hope that he would be re-elected. Father Vattmann also visited a large number of the parishes of the State, and told the clergy what McKinley had said to the A. P. A. committee. When the election was held in November, McKinley received 81,995 plurality.

His tremendous change from 21,511 to 81,995

greatly enhanced his chances for the Presidential nomination in 1896.

Later, in 1903, Captain Vattmann did great service in settling the religious question in the Philippines, but I will tell that story later, in an interview at Oyster Bay with Roosevelt.

V

MARK HANNA AND CHARLES G. DAWES

DURING the winter of 1894 the work of securing McKinley delegates in the Middle West became too heavy for the small group of men Mr. Hanna had chosen to work with him. During one of his visits to Chicago he stopped at the Wellington Hotel, now the site of Lyon & Healy's music store. We dined together, and he told me a young fellow whose father, General Rufus Dawes, was Major McKinley's old commander, had been to see him and had offered his services. Mr. Hanna had asked the young man to come to the hotel that evening. While we were in Mr. Hanna's room he was announced, a rather pale, slight figure, and somewhat diffident. We discussed plans with him, as he displayed great interest in McKinley's success and offered his services free of all expense. After he left the room Mr. Hanna remarked: "He doesn't *look* much, does he?" I said: "Any man who will work for nothing and pay his own expenses looks good to me!"

One would hardly recognize the "pale, slight figure" of 1894 in the brilliant officer, Brigadier-General Charles G. Dawes, whose splendid record during the war won him the confidence of our Allies and justified General Pershing's faith in him. He displayed no "diffidence" when he appeared before a congressional committee last spring and made "Hell and Maria" famous, and later in his "lecture" to cabinet officers and department chiefs whose co-operation he asked when he drew up the first national budget for President Harding.

"Charlie" Dawes, as his friends call him, devoted himself to the McKinley cause. He initiated a card-index system extending from the Alleghanies to the Pacific, and probably, next to Mr. Hanna, did more to win the nomination for McKinley at St. Louis than any other man.

VI

McKINLEY AT THOMASVILLE, GA.

EARLY in 1895 Governor and Mrs. McKinley visited Mr. and Mrs. Hanna in Thomasville, Ga. Mrs. McKinley was always delicate, and the cold weather aggravated her illness, so the governor gladly accepted the Hanna invitation, and Mr. and Mrs. Myron T. Herrick, my family and myself joined them in the hospitable Hanna home. Mr. Hanna sent for a number of the Republican leaders in the Southern States and had them meet McKinley, one or two at a time, in the beautiful sun parlor of the house.

I think, without exception, they were delighted with the governor, and pledged him their support in 1896, and most of them kept their pledge.

The Atlanta *Constitution*, edited by my good friend Clark Howell, got wind of the visits of the politicians and had his correspondents sending daily accounts of the meetings. Some of the comments were unfavorable, which was natural in an opposition paper. I wrote Mr. Howell and invited him to come to Thomasville and meet McKinley and Hanna. He did so, and from that day his paper and he, personally, were extremely kind to the governor, without in any way changing his political policy.

The friendship lasted until McKinley's death.

I will depart from the thread of my story to tell of President McKinley's visit to Atlanta in 1898, but let Mr. Howell tell his own story as he wrote it:

Atlanta, Ga.,
December 22, 1921.

MY DEAR KOHLSAAT:

The McKinley incident as I recall it, is as follows:

President McKinley came to Atlanta as the chief guest of honor at a Peace Jubilee banquet given under the auspices of Atlanta businessmen in the fall following the close of the Spanish-American War in 1898, at which banquet I presided.

During the morning of his arrival here, his secretary, Mr. Cortelyou, made a call on me at my office, stating that the president wished to see me at the Kimball House.

I went there and was ushered into the private parlor with the statement that "the president is shaving but he will be glad to see you."

Only President and Mrs. McKinley were in the room when I went in. She was sitting before an open fire with a shawl thrown lightly around her shoulders. The president sat before a glass at a table in the centre of the room. A towel was around his neck, his face was lathered, and he was shaving himself.

He welcomed me stating that he had sent for me to read the address he had prepared to deliver to the General Assembly then in session in Atlanta, before which he had been invited to speak that day at noon.

He handed me the address, which I proceeded to read.

Every once in a while he left his table and walked to

the side of his frail wife, solicitously fastening the shawl around her shoulders, patting her on the cheek and returning to his conversation with me.

"The feature of the address that I want you to see," said he, "is the reference to the government care of the Confederate graves," in which he stated in referring to the complete reconciliation between the sections, that the time had come when the Federal Government should take over the care of the graves of Confederate veterans.

My father, a Confederate veteran, was then a member of the committee that had been appointed by the president to investigate charges growing out of government purchases during the Spanish-American War.

About a month before this, in a letter to my father I had suggested that if President McKinley, who had just accepted the invitation to speak in Atlanta, would make an expression in favor of the government's caring for Confederate graves, he would strike a very responsive key note. My father had written me that he had shown my letter to the president who seemed pleased with the suggestion.

I thought no more of it until the president submitted his address to me.

I went with the president to the joint session of the General Assembly that day. The galleries were crowded and every member of both houses arose as the president was escorted to the speaker's stand. He was given a very cordial ovation, for while differing with him politically, the South held McKinley in high personal esteem.

There was nothing unusual about the first few minutes of his address. He was mildly applauded from time to time as he said something that caught his audience.

After a while he reached that part of his address referring to the care of Confederate graves by the government. He had purposely held it as a climax.

In a minute the audience was in a storm of applause.

I never before witnessed such a scene in our General Assembly. Both the galleries and the floor joined in an uproar of enthusiasm. Every person in the hall stood and every handkerchief went up into the air.

Tears flowed down the cheeks of Confederate veterans and when the president concluded, they, particularly, made a rush to shake his hand.

He saw instantly that he had caught the heart of his audience and he seemed to be immensely pleased at the result.

As we left, he said "They liked it, didn't they?"

The speech caught the whole South and the next day was the talk of the town.

This covers the incident as I recall it. It was a long time ago but it is still fresh in my memory.

And the one thing about that day that I will never forget and that has always endeared McKinley's memory to me was the beautiful, sweet solicitude of this strong, manly man to his sweet, frail wife as she sat by the fireside that day.

With cordial personal regards and best wishes, I am

Sincerely yours,

(Signed.) CLARK HOWELL.

Joseph Medill, of the Chicago *Tribune*, was also in Thomasville in 1895 and joined in some of the conferences. His grandson, Medill McCormick, spent a few weeks with him and sent in some of his first efforts as a cub reporter to *The Tribune*. I think he met his future wife, Miss Ruth Hanna, the apple of Mark Hanna's eye, during this visit. I met them riding in the pine-woods many times—the slim, dark-eyed Ruth in a trim riding-habit, riding astride a high-mettled horse. It was said she could control any of the spirited horses of Thomasville, for which the city was famous.

When McKinley left for Columbus, I rode as far as Atlanta with him and visited my friends Clark Howell, Joel Chandler Harris, and Frank L. Stanton for a few days.

"Uncle Remus" invited me to a noon meal at his home. When we arrived at the front gate he said in that wonderful musical voice of his: "Mr. Kohlsaat, would you mind our going around to the kitchen gate? A little wren has built her nest in this gate-post, so we boarded it up until the little birds are hatched."

VII

McKINLEY, TOM PLATT, AND MARK HANNA

AFTER selling *The Inter-Ocean* in March, 1894, with my family I spent several months in Europe. On our return we lived in Washington for a few weeks in the fall of 1894, going to Thomasville in the winter of 1895.

While in Washington in March, 1895, I secured a provisional option on a number of shares of the New York *Times* from Mr. Charles R. Flint. A block of stock necessary to obtain complete control was not obtainable for some months, so the purchase was never completed. During the negotiations for the purchase of the New York *Times*, my boyhood friend James W. Scott purchased the Chicago *Herald* from John R. Walsh and the Chicago *Times* from other parties, and merged them into the Chicago *Times-Herald*. He also bought *The Evening Post* from Mr. Walsh.

On April 22, 1895, sixty days after he had acquired the papers, Mr. Scott died suddenly in the Holland House, New York.

Thirty days later I purchased his holdings in both

papers and changed *The Times-Herald* from a Democratic to a Republican newspaper. *The Evening Post* was independent and remained so.

A year after my purchase of *The Times-Herald* the New York *Times* people wrote they could now deliver the control. I wrote them it was too late. A few days later my friend Adolph S. Ochs, owner of the Chattanooga *Times*, was at lunch with me in the Chicago Club, and told me he had the New York *Times* under consideration. I told him it was the opportunity of his life, and urged him strongly to take hold of it. To this Mr. Ochs protested that he didn't think he was a big enough man for the job. I replied: "Don't tell anybody and perhaps they'll never find out." I gave him a letter to Mr. Charles R. Flint, with whom I had discussed the purchase of *The Times*. After months of negotiation *The Times* was turned over to Mr. Ochs with full control, August 18, 1896.

Colonel Edward M. House told me a few weeks ago he was at luncheon this summer with J. St. Loe Strachey, proprietor and editor of the London *Spectator*—one of England's foremost editors. They were discussing English and American newspapers. Mr. Strachey said: "Since boyhood I have looked on the London *Times* as the greatest newspaper in the world, but I now believe the New York *Times* occupies that place." Evidently Mr. Ochs did not tell what he thought of his newspaper abilities and proved that he *was* big enough to run the New York *Times*.

During the year 1895 there were frequent meetings, held generally in Cleveland, of McKinley, Hanna, Herrick, and myself. At one of the gatherings Hanna was asked to go to New York and try to interest Thomas C. Platt and Matt Quay, of Pennsylvania, in McKinley's candidacy. One Sunday some weeks later in the Hanna home we were sitting in what Mr. Hanna called his "den"; after dinner, when McKinley asked Hanna what report he had to make of his visit to Platt and Quay, Hanna said: "You can get both New York and Pennsylvania, Governor, but there are certain conditions." McKinley asked: "What are they?" Hanna replied: "They want a promise that you will appoint Tom Platt Secretary of the Treasury, and they want it in writing. Platt says he has had an experience with one President (Harrison) born in Ohio, and he wants no more verbal promises." McKinley was smoking a cigar. He threw his head back and let the smoke curl up for a moment or so, then got up and paced the little room for a few minutes; finally, facing Hanna, Herrick, and me, he said: "There are some things in this world that come too high. If I cannot be President without promising to make Tom Platt Secretary of the Treasury, I will never be President." Hanna remarked: "New York and

SENATOR HANNA

Pennsylvania will clinch the nomination—with the votes already in sight." McKinley said: "I can't do it, Mark." "Well," sighed Hanna, "we have got to work harder to make up that big block of votes, but we will get them!"

At a later meeting held in the Herrick home in Prospect Street, while we and our wives were at dinner, the maid notified Mr. Herrick that two gentlemen wanted to see him in the parlor. Herrick excused himself. A few minutes later we heard some loud talk and then a slam of the front door. Herrick, flushed and mad, returned to the dining-room. Mark Hanna asked who they were. Herrick said: "A couple of blackmailers!"

It seems they have a law in Ohio giving half to an informer of securities not listed for taxation. These two men told Herrick he had some loans in his bank, The Society for Savings, on securities that had not been listed. He asked to see the paper, containing the names and securities, which he quietly put in his pocket. They raised a row and it looked serious for a few minutes, until Herrick put them out. They could see McKinley and Hanna from the hall, as the house was small, and probably thought "discretion was the better part of valor." A little later, when Herrick was not in the room, McKinley said: "You would not think Myron had the nerve to do that, would you?" But since he notified the German

Government in August, 1914, without consulting the State Department at Washington, that "Every American and his property would be protected in Paris," and stayed at his post and took over the British, Russian and Belgian embassies, as their ministers left hurriedly, anything can be expected of what McKinley called "Myron's nerve."

VIII

THE ST. LOUIS CONVENTION OF 1896

In May, 1896, a mutual friend informed me that the policy of *The Times-Herald* greatly embarrassed Mr. Hanna. The paper continually insisted on a clear declaration for gold at St. Louis.

As the majority of the McKinley delegates were from the Middle West and West, Mr. Hanna was bombarded with the question: "Who represents Mr. McKinley, you or *The Times-Herald,* on the money question?" I was told that Mr. Hanna replied: "Kohlsaat is a crank and does not represent anybody but himself."

Without any previous understanding, Mr. Hanna and I had no communication for some two months before the convention, which was called for June 16.

Sunday, June 7, I went to Canton, Ohio, and spent eight hours with McKinley, urging him to declare definitely for gold. He told me that 90 per cent of his correspondence and callers assured him it would defeat him to do so. He said Whitelaw Reid, editor of the New York *Tribune,* had been to see him a few days before, on his return from Arizona to New York, and strongly advised against it. Reid said: "If a gold plank is adopted we will not carry a State west of the Mississippi River."

On Mr. Reid's return to New York, *The Tribune* printed the following editorial:

There is no occasion to maintain that the words "Gold Standard" must of necessity be used, because the present standard is that, and everybody knows it, etc., etc.

I received a telegram from Alexander H. Revell, of Chicago, dated St. Louis, June 11, '96: "If you want to see the word 'gold' in the plank, you should come down here." So left that night, and on arrival about 10 o'clock Friday, the 12th, I went to the McKinley headquarters. Outside the door I met Raymond Patterson, Washington correspondent of the Chicago *Tribune*. He said: "Every man that goes into that room for gold comes out for silver."

In the room were Mark Hanna, Myron T. Herrick, Henry C. Payne, Melville E. Stone, ex-Governor Merriam, of Minnesota, and Senator Redfield Proctor, of Vermont.

Mr. Payne handed me a copy of a plank that had been agreed upon and approved by McKinley.

After leaving Canton the word "gold" had been inserted between "existing" and "standard" and then crossed out again, making it read: "The existing standard must be maintained."

Mr. Hanna explained the plank had been changed because there was strong protest against the word "gold" from Indiana, Michigan, Iowa, Nebraska, and other States west of the Mississippi, where the majority of the McKinley delegates were to come from.

I argued it was cowardice not to say "gold" and make the declaration definite; that the plank they had adopted meant gold to the gold-man and silver to the silver-man. Mr. Hanna insisted it might defeat McKinley's nomination if the word "gold" was put in.

We made little headway for an hour or so. Finally Hanna said: "Damn you, Herman, haven't you any compromise in your make-up?" I replied: "Not on this issue, Mark." "Well," he said, "I have no more time to waste on a damned crank," and left the room.

About 3 o'clock, after five hours of argument, the hated word was put between existing and standard. Mark Hanna was sent for and told what had been agreed upon. He turned to me and said: "Are you satisfied now, you damned crank?" I said: "Yes; I don't like the promise to send a commission to Europe to work for bimetallism, but will stand for it."

We then pledged ourselves not to give publicity to the plank, as it would upset the McKinley delegates that were for silver.

After the meeting Mr. Hanna asked me to come to his room, and, holding both my hands, he said: "You probably have noticed I have dropped you entirely for a couple of months. Well, I want to tell you I am just as strong a gold-man as you are, but if I had been as outspoken as you we would not have gotten the votes for McKinley, but I want you to know I love you just as much as ever."

He then told me they had over 530 votes pledged for McKinley, and it took only 463 to nominate him. McKinley actually received 564, which was 100 more than necessary in a total of 924 in the convention. The gold plank received 812½ votes and the silver 110½.

There has been much discussion as to who wrote the gold plank. It was sent out after its adoption by the convention by the Associated Press and others as "the Kohlsaat plank," but I had nothing whatever to do with writing the plank, except to put the word "gold" between the words "existing" and "standard." Every one of the seven men present was a strong gold advocate, but some feared it would defeat McKinley if the offensive word was put into the platform; with the exception of Senator Proctor, they were all from the Middle West. They had complete control of the convention, and could have passed any plank agreed upon. With a few changes in wording and the addition of the word "gold" it was the plank agreed upon by Governor McKinley in Canton ten days before the convention, and was taken to St. Louis by Mark Hanna.

Saturday, the 13th, I mailed a copy of the plank to Horace White, editor of the New York *Evening Post*, and asked him not to publish it, but to wire me if he approved it. Tuesday morning his reply came: "The financial plank is satisfactory to me."

Monday, June 15, I was in Mr. Hanna's room in the Southern Hotel when Senator Lodge, who arrived in St. Louis Sunday afternoon, came in, and walked to the table where Mr. Hanna was reading the speech of the temporary chairman of the convention, Charles W. Fairbanks. Without any preliminary greeting Mr. Lodge said: "Mr. Hanna, I insist on a positive declaration for a gold-standard plank in the platform." Hanna looked up and said: "Who in hell are you?" Lodge answered: "Senator Henry Cabot Lodge, of Massachusetts." "Well, Senator Henry Cabot Lodge, of Massachusetts, you can go plumb to hell. You have nothing to say about it," replied Mr. Hanna. Lodge said: "All right, sir; I will make my fight on the floor of the convention." "I don't care a damn where you make your fight," replied Hanna.

After Lodge left the room I said: "Mark, you made a mistake. We don't want a fight on our hands. Let me show Lodge the plank we agreed on last Friday." Hanna replied: "You can't trust that blankety-blank man; he will give the plank to the press." I again said: "Let me show it to him and tell him how important it is to keep it quiet, so as not to have a silver bolt in the convention." Hanna said: "All right, but you do it on your own responsibility."

So I went to the Massachusetts headquarters, which were in the same hotel, found Lodge, introduced myself and told him I had heard the tilt between him and Hanna; that he must not resent Mr. Hanna's attitude, as he had had but little sleep for a week, and then told him of the Friday meeting and showed him the plank agreed upon by the McKinley managers, and of our pledge of no-publicity. He read it and said: "Why, that plank is all right; the only change I would make is to knock out the words 'and unlimited' in the sentence 'we are opposed to the free and unlimited coinage of silver.' The two words are unnecessary."

I made the change and have the paper framed. The only words that have not faded out of the mimeograph copy are the word "gold" and "out suggestion of Lodge," both written in pencil.

Lodge asked me for a copy. I said: "I cannot give it to you." He replied: "I want to show it especially to one man who is going to make a fight on the floor. I will keep it confidential."

I was weak enough to consent and his stenographer copied it. This happened Monday morning about 11 o'clock.

The evening papers of Tuesday in St. Louis printed

a despatch from Boston giving the contents of the plank I had handed Lodge. About 6 o'clock that evening I met Mr. Hanna in the hall. He was very angry and said: "Have you seen the evening papers? I told you you could not trust that blankety-blank-blank, and if the premature publication causes a break in the McKinley ranks, you are responsible."

Fortunately, but few saw the despatch, as the papers did not put a display head on it; they were too full of local happenings to "play up" outside news. The only man outside Mr. Hanna to make a protest to me when he read the Boston despatch was Mr. M. H. De Young, owner of the San Francisco *Chronicle*. He said: "California would not stand for the gold standard." I reminded him that California was more interested in a protective tariff on citrous fruits than a money standard! The California papers during the campaign that followed soft-pedalled the money question and strongly approved the tariff plank.

Afterward one of the Boston correspondents told me Lodge gave him the plank and said: "That is what I stand for!"

He did not claim he wrote it, but a week later he was introduced at the Harvard Convocation exercises as the author of the gold plank, and, as the papers reported, "received a great ovation"!

He made no denial.

Two or three days later Senator Proctor sent me a despatch (which I have) asking me to send him a wire which he could print and read to his audiences telling of the writing of the gold plank Friday, June 12. He said: "Give me as much credit as you can, as other Eastern men are claiming authorship."

In an interview sent out by the Associated Press, June 5, 1922, Senator Lodge denied he had received from me a copy of the Gold Plank adopted by the McKinley managers, June 12, 1896.

If the senator from Massachusetts will read page 325 of "The Autobiography of Thomas Collier Platt," senator from New York, written in 1910, he will find the following paragraph:

"That night Governor Merriam came to Mr. Platt, and Mr. Kohlsaat went to Senator Lodge with a draft of the original Hanna Plank with the word 'Gold' inserted," etc.

The "original Hanna Plank" was written Friday, June 12, 1896, and was accepted that night by Governor McKinley after a long-distance telephone talk with Melville E. Stone and Myron T. Herrick.

Senator Lodge says he arrived in St. Louis Sunday, June 14, two days later. Consequently, he had no hand in "forcing Mr. Hanna to accept the word 'Gold.'"

IX

MELVILLE E. STONE—FIFTY YEARS A JOURNALIST

MELVILLE E. STONE, general manager of the Associated Press in 1896, was present during the conference of the McKinley managers in the Southern Hotel, June 12, 1896, when the "gold"-standard plank was written.

Mr. Stone, in his interesting book "Fifty Years a Journalist," writes as follows:

The "Major," as we called McKinley in those days, was a friend. Four or five days before the St. Louis Convention he had asked me to come to his home at Canton, and I went there. We sat for a long afternoon on the porch of his cottage. He had received at the hands of Mr. Robert W. Patterson, managing editor of the Chicago *Tribune*, a proposed plank for the platform to be adopted at the St. Louis Convention. It referred to the monetary question and declared in a modified way for bimetallism. I was president of the Globe National Bank of Chicago at the time, and he did me the honour to ask my view of Patterson's proposal. I promptly told him that there was no such thing as bimetallism possible. I used the well-known illustration of the yardstick, and assured him that two yardsticks of different length could not be. In truth, Major McKinley had no settled opinion in respect of the matter, and he said he was convinced that the financial question would, after all, not be the issue of the coming campaign. I challenged this view, and, having in mind some things that had happened, said that neither he nor the National Convention could determine the issue, and that the people would in the end do this. Finally, he told me that Charles Emory Smith was drafting the platform, and he asked me to see him in St. Louis and try to settle the matter.

The thing that had happened, and which forced me to believe that the silver question and not the tariff was to be the issue, was the action of the Peoria Convention of the Democratic Party in Illinois, which had already been held. The controlling force in that convention was a very astute politician, Governor John P. Altgeld of Chicago. He had thrust the issue of bimetallism into the Peoria Convention and secured the passage of a resolution declaring for a 16-to-1 standard. But for the fact that he was born in Germany, and therefore ineligible to the office of President of the United States, it is not unlikely that he would have been the national Democratic candidate that year.

The story of the adoption of the gold-standard plank at the Republican National Convention has frequently been told, yet not always accurately. When I arrived in St. Louis I found a good deal of confusion. I was called into a conference of Major McKinley's friends. Those present were H. H. Kohlsaat, editor of the Chicago *Times-Herald*, ex-Governor W. R. Merriam of Minnesota; the Hon. Myron T. Herrick of Ohio; Senator Redfield Proctor of Vermont; the Hon. Henry C. Payne of Milwaukee, and Mark Hanna. As manager for the McKinley forces,

Mr. Hanna found himself in a difficult position. Several Western states were earnestly for free-silver coinage. Mr. Hanna, therefore, while personally a gold-standard man, was unwilling to take the responsibility of actively participating in the fight against a declaration for bimetallism. After repeated conferences a resolution committing the Republican Party to the gold standard was agreed to. The most urgent and uncompromising advocate of a gold plank was Mr. Kohlsaat. My only part in the framing of the plank was to write in the word "inviolable" in the pledge to "maintain (inviolable) the obligations of the United States at the existing standard."

After the wording of the resolution had been finally agreed upon, it was necessary to submit it to Major McKinley. A long-distance telephone-line between the Southern Hotel in St. Louis and the McKinley cottage in Canton had been established, and Mr. Hanna and I went to the St. Louis end of the wire in the basement of the hotel to read the plank to the waiting candidate at Canton. It was a new experience for Mr. Hanna, and he could not make himself heard. I therefore read the resolution. Major McKinley asked if that had been fully agreed upon by his friends, to which I replied that it had. Reluctantly he acquiesced in it, but asked if it was not possible to introduce a modifying phrase pledging the Republican party to promote an international agreement for the free coinage of silver. In obedience to this suggestion such a phrase was introduced, and the plank was later adopted by the convention.

Mr. McKinley's campaign, carried on from his cottage at Canton, was a remarkable one. Although he had never given the financial question very serious consideration, and certainly had no adequate conception of the business when nominated, he delivered speech after speech of such cogency as to command the attention and admiration of every student of finance.

X

LETTER TO HORACE WHITE—1896

In 1912 Horace White, editor of the New York
Evening Post, wrote he was clearing up his papers at
eighty, and was returning to me the following letter
I wrote July 1, 1896, ten days after the convention,
as he thought "it would be interesting after sixteen
years":

July 1, 1896.

Horace White Esq.,
The Evening Post,
N. Y. City.

My dear Mr. White,

I have just read the enclosed article taken from *The
Evening Post* of Monday, June 29th. I do not know Mr.
Angell and never heard of him, but he is evidently a friend
of Mr. Herrick and the plank was probably sent to him
by Mr. Herrick. The article is correct in every way, excepting that Senator Lodge saw the plank as you have it
printed on the Monday morning. He said it suited him
perfectly with the one exception that he would strike out
the two words "and unlimited." He thought that the
plank would be stronger if it read "we are opposed to
the free coinage of silver." He said that was all the
change he would make and asked me for a copy of the
plank. I handed him the copy I now enclose to you.
His secretary struck off copies and I understand that Mr.
Lodge took them to different eastern men and said that
they had been given him by one of Governor McKinley's
closest friends, that it was the plank that had been agreed

upon by the McKinley management and that would be presented to the committee on resolutions. The original phraseology of the plank is to a large extent McKinley's own excepting that his plank read "The Republican party caused the enactment of the law providing for the resumption of specie payment in 1879. Since then every dollar has been as good as gold and we pledge ourselves to keep it so." It was thought that it would be stronger to say that "we believed the existing gold standard should be preserved" and so Governor McKinley's draft was changed. On Thursday, June 11th, the leading Republicans of Michigan, Indiana, Iowa and Nebraska protested against using the word "gold" in the platform. They said that it would need a great amount of explanation to their constituents—that the free coinage people would claim that it meant the abolishment of silver and paper money and that nothing but gold would be in circulation. On Friday in the conference the plank read "We believe the existing standard should be maintained." This was done because of the earnest appeals of men from the states I have mentioned. Of course the gold standard could not win if the electoral vote from those states was lost; consequently their appeals had great weight. There were seven in the conference and they thought it was perhaps unnecessary to slap the voters of the middle western states in the face by inserting the word "gold" contrary to their wishes. I took the position that it was cowardice not to put the word "gold" in because that was what the words "existing standard" meant and I said that we had better have a straight-out fight and avoid dodging. The conference lasted five hours and at the end of that time the word was put in as you see it in this original copy. Our mutual friend Mr. M. E. Stone is responsible for the change which reads "to the extent only as its parity with gold can be maintained" and also for the word "inviolably." In the last line you will see that the word "standard" occurs twice—"at the present standard, the standard of the most enlightened nations of the earth." This was the suggestion of Senator Proctor of Vermont, a warm friend of McKinley and the only eastern man in the conference. The senator remarked at the time he put it in that the strongest words possible should be used as every word in the plank ought to weigh a ton.

I have been somewhat surprised at the claims of Senator Lodge and Mr. Platt that the East dictated the plank, for they know this to be absolutely false. I have always looked upon Lodge as a pretty decent sort of a man, but he surely does not add any lustre to his name by attempting to appropriate what belongs to others. The McKinley managers had 564 votes (100 more than was necessary), to pass a plank which would simply declare against the free coinage of silver and in favor of maintaining the existing standard. They also could have adopted what is known as the Indiana plank. The 238 votes of New England, New York and Pennsylvania were simply added to the majority which McKinley already controlled.

You will notice that in McKinley's speech to the notification committee he took occasion to say that the people did not complain of the administration borrowing money and issuing bonds to preserve our credit, which means that he would do what he told me a week ago he would do, viz. use all the power vested in the chief executive to maintain the treasury reserve. He said "I have no sympathy with the demagogic appeals to the prejudices of the people against Cleveland issuing bonds; he did what every patriotic man should do and nothing but his duty." He told me that if the Republican party should be successful at the polls in November it would be their first duty upon coming into power to adopt measures to provide suffi-

cient revenue to run the government and pay off its in-
debtedness—that he would not give out an office until
he had satisfactory legislation and until such legislation
could become operative he would use all the power vested
in the President to maintain the gold reserve.   There is
no necessity for his coming out and saying so at this
time, for I assure you, Mr. White, we have a battle on
our hands in this section of the country and McKinley
must do nothing to detract from his personal popularity,
for that is one of the strongest factors of his success.   I
honestly believe that if Mr. Morton had been nominated
on a gold platform it would have been impossible for us
to carry Illinois against Altgeld and free silver.   Altgeld
is extremely strong with the labor people and Tanner, the
Republican nominee, is so thoroughly unfit for the position that decent, God-fearing people are almost in open
revolt against him.

Please return this original draft of the plank as I wish
to have it framed and preserve it.   I would not part with
it for considerable money.

Yours sincerely,

(Signed) H. H. KOHLSAAT.

The New York *Evening Post* printed several editorials in 1896 ridiculing the claims of Platt and
Lodge that they wrote the gold plank.

XI

THE PRESIDENTIAL CAMPAIGN OF 1896

In July, 1896, the Democratic national convention met in Chicago. The dominant figure was Governor John P. Altgeld, of Illinois. Born in Germany, he was ineligible for the Presidency, or would in all probability have been the nominee. He was an ardent advocate of free silver, and, as the Democratic State convention, held at Peoria a few weeks before, instructed the delegates to the national convention to vote for free silver by something like 1,000 to 3 votes for gold, Altgeld had the backing of his party in Illinois for his heresy.

The great speech of the convention was made by a handsome, virile young fellow, William Jennings Bryan, of Nebraska; his "cross of gold" speech set the convention wild.

Major Moses P. Handy, chief of the editorial page of *The Times-Herald,* on his return from the hall, came into my room in great excitement, and said he had just heard the greatest speech of his life, and predicted Bryan's nomination next day. Bryan was almost unknown until he made his speech. Few of the newspapers had photographs of him. *The Times-*

Herald was fortunate enough to have a very good one. I sent for Mr. Von Hofsten, our best pen-sketch artist, and asked him to make a five-column drawing of Bryan, and do his best. It was printed on the front page under the caption "Probable Nominee To-day's Convention," running across seven columns. About 5 o'clock next morning some of Bryan's friends ordered 5,000 copies, which they took to the convention hall. They pinned them on their breasts and fastened them to brooms, and marched round and round the hall, headed by a band, yelling: "Bryan, Bryan, William Jennings Bryan!"

Mr. Bryan told me later he thought the picture had a lot to do with his receiving the nomination, and asked for the original drawing, which was sent to Mrs. Bryan.

The campaign was probably the most exciting in the history of the country; there were street parades almost daily, and at noon and night the busy corners of the down-town streets were filled by crowds listening to free-silver orators standing on soap-boxes.

All outward appearances indicated that silver would win, and good political judges predicted Illinois would give 100,000 majority for Bryan, but second sober thought prevailed and McKinley carried the State by something like 160,000.

Millions of pamphlets written in simple language

were sent broadcast showing the fallacy of free silver.

The campaign committees sent out some 2,000,000 copies of a pamphlet entitled "A Free Coinage Catechism," written by Alexander Dana Noyes, at that time financial editor of the New York *Evening Post*, at present holding the same position on the New York *Times* and also financial editor of *Scribner's Magazine*. Mr. Noyes's pamphlet was widely read East and West, and was a very effective guide for public speakers.

Another pamphlet, written by George E. Roberts, of Iowa, was a complete answer to "Coin's Financial School," a book which was the most dangerous weapon in the free-silver arsenal. The committee sent millions of copies of Mr. Roberts's pamphlets throughout the Middle and Western States.

When Lyman J. Gage became Secretary of the Treasury in McKinley's cabinet, he asked the President to appoint Mr. Roberts director of the mint. He was reappointed by both Roosevelt and Taft. He is now vice-president of the National City Bank, New York City.

Leslie M. Shaw, governor of Iowa, and later Secretary of the Treasury in Roosevelt's cabinet, was a strong advocate of the gold standard. His plain, homely speeches to the farmers comparing our financial system to the "lean-to" so familiar to the average farmhouse brought about a change of sentiment from free silver to gold.

He probably did more than any other man to carry Iowa for McKinley.

The silver-mine owners contributed a huge sum to the campaign and paid for the circulation of a book called "Coin," written by a man named Harvey. It was written simply and quoted treasury figures, which to many were unanswerable. I paid Harvey to write a column a day, reserving the right to print a parallel column in reply. Professor J. Laurence Laughlin, professor of political economy in the University of Chicago, answered Harvey's arguments daily. After the articles had been running less than a week, Harvey came to see me and asked who was answering him. He was told Professor Laughlin. He declined to go on with his contract.

Governor Altgeld delivered a speech in the Auditorium. The house was packed. I read his speech while he was delivering it. He made such a strong argument I telephoned Professor Laughlin to come to the office. After reading Altgeld's effort he said: "If the governor's figures of the condition of the treasury were correct, the speech is unanswerable, but he has deliberately lied and given false figures."

The Times-Herald printed the speech in full, but put Professor Laughlin's short statement in a box at the head of the column. A few days later I met

Altgeld in a street-car. He said: "Kohlsaat, that was a dirty trick you played on me."

The gold-standard people organized parades all over the country. Toward the end of October heads of business houses, bank presidents, and men of large affairs, Democrats and Republicans, tramped miles through the streets, followed by their employees. As Election day drew near, business was paralyzed —the banks declined to make loans—fear took possession of the business community. Every voter was called upon to go to the polls.

Election night the streets near the newspaper offices were packed. When the returns at midnight indicated McKinley's election, the clubs and hotels were filled with excited men. There was no prohibition. Volstead was unknown.

Long after midnight in a certain Chicago club one of the world's greatest merchants started the old boyhood game "Follow the Leader." He was joined by bank presidents, merchants, Chicago's foremost men; they went over sofas, chairs, tables, up-stairs and down-stairs, and wound up with dancing in each other's arms.

A little after midnight I rang up McKinley in Canton. His nephew, James McKinley, answered the phone. I asked him to let me speak to the President-elect. After some minutes' wait young McKinley said: "I found Uncle Will in his mother's room.

The old lady is kneeling beside the bed with one arm around the governor and the other around Aunt Ida, praying. All I heard was: 'Oh, God, keep him humble.'"

XII

McKINLEY CHOOSING HIS CABINET

Two weeks after his nomination at St. Louis the notification committee went to Canton and addressed McKinley on the porch of his modest two-story cottage. His acceptance speech reassured the country, as he stood squarely on the gold platform. About ten days later I was on a Pennsylvania train going from New York to Canton and met Mr. Hobart, the Vice-Presidential nominee. He was going to read his acceptance speech to McKinley before receiving his notification committee.

After breakfast in the McKinley home we went to an attic room. It was bare of furniture, with the exception of a plain pine table and one chair. Mr. Hobart occupied the chair. McKinley and I sat on the edge of the table, dangling our legs. As Hobart read his letter of acceptance we both made suggestions. McKinley ripped it to pieces, so that when Hobart returned to New York, it bore little resemblance to the letter he brought to Canton.

During the next few weeks Canton was the centre of attraction to the newspaper correspondents.

Mr. Hanna, Mr. Herrick, Colonel John Hay, and

other close friends were weekly visitors.   McKinley was very solicitous as to who should be Secretary of the Treasury.   It is not generally known that Mark Hanna wanted that portfolio, but McKinley hesitated; first, because it would look too much like paying a political debt and, second, because he did not think Hanna had the training necessary.   He said to me: "I don't think Mark knows enough about governmental finance to fill the position."

Nelson Dingley, of Maine, author of the Dingley Bill, was offered and accepted the Secretary of the Treasury post.   Along about the end of January, 1897, McKinley rang me up one Saturday night in my home, and told me he had received a letter from Dingley saying his doctor had told him if he took the treasury post he would not live two years, and his family insisted that he give it up.   He asked to be released.   McKinley said: "That knocks my cabinet into a cocked hat; I was building it around the Secretary of the Treasury."

The papers published the news of Dingley's declination the next morning.

It occurred to me that Lyman J. Gage would be an ideal man for the place.   He was president of the First National Bank of Chicago, a gold Democrat, and well known to the bankers of the entire country. I called on him Sunday afternoon and suggested it to him.   He shook his head and said: "I have no political ambition." I answered: "That is just why you should take the place if offered. The country is nervous over the money question, and faith in the man to be at the head of the treasury is vital. Mc-Kinley knows nothing of finance. He has been weak on the silver question, and confidence is of supreme importance, especially at this critical period."

But he was obdurate.

That night our neighbor, O. W. Potter, gave a dinner to Sol Smith Russell, the comedian, and his wife. My wife and I were invited; so were Mr. and Mrs. Gage. I took Mrs. Gage out to dinner and told her of my visit to her husband that afternoon. She was greatly interested as I drew a picture of a cabinet officer's social position. Before we separated I had a friend at court.

Next morning Mr. Gage and I walked to business together. I urged him to reconsider. He said: "Why should I give up a perfectly easy job with $25,000 salary to accept one at $8,000 and spend three times my salary to live in Washington?"

Next morning we walked again. I noticed signs of weakening. Mrs. Gage had evidently been at work! As we parted I said: "When you get to your office send me a note by messenger and tell me just what you will do." An hour later I received the note, which read: "After thinking of the matter I

cannot *at present* give you the answer you want."
The underlining of "at present" convinced me that
he did not want to say that he would accept a position that had not been offered to him. So I rang
up Governor McKinley at Canton and said: "I have
a Secretary of the Treasury for you."

"Who is it?"

"Lyman J. Gage, president of the First National
Bank. A gold Democrat. He will represent the
gold Democrats in your cabinet. His appointment
will show appreciation for their votes, as you would
have been defeated without them."

"Have I ever met him?"

"Yes, you met him at a reception given by Ferdi-
nand W. Peck on Ohio Day, at the World's Fair in
1893."

"Did he have white whiskers?"

"Yes."

"Oh, I remember him.   Hold the wire a moment.
That is an inspiration.   Let me think."

After two or three minutes McKinley said: "I
will send Charlie Dawes to see him Thursday.   Pre-
pare him for the visit."

The next morning the papers announced that great
pressure was being brought to bear on Governor Mc-
Kinley to appoint Lyman J. Gage, of Chicago, Secretary of the Treasury. Mark Hanna came from
Cleveland to Canton and said: "Where in hell is the

great pressure? I never heard him mentioned for the place!"

McKinley told me afterward he received more telegrams and letters of commendation on Gage's appointment than all the other cabinet places combined.

Colonel John J. McCook had been slated for Attorney-General and Judge Joseph McKenna, of California, for Secretary of the Interior.

McKinley had a way of throwing out names for cabinet places, and watching the reaction. If the man met with approval, he sent for him. If the suggestion stirred up opposition, he was dropped.

When Judge McKenna, now Justice McKenna of the U. S. Supreme Court, was suggested, the California papers were unstinted in their praise of him both as a judge and congressman. McKinley sent for McKenna to come to Canton. On his arrival he lunched in the McKinley cottage. McKinley told me the following story of the McKenna appointment:

"'Well, judge, they have been pretty busy with your name lately for a cabinet post.' McKenna replied: 'Yes, governor, but I don't believe you realize what you are doing. I am a Roman Catholic, and the Protestants will never permit a Catholic to have charge of the Indian Missions.'" McKinley continued: "Without taking my eyes from his, I said: 'The place I want you for, judge, has nothing to do with the Indian Missions. I want you for Attorney-General.' 'Oh, I was misinformed,' said McKenna. 'If you see fit to tender me that honor, I accept with pleasure.'"

Later McKinley laughingly said: "I don't believe the judge suspected that I switched him! We were in Congress together several years, and it never occurred to me that he was a Catholic!"

Next day the papers announced McKenna was to be Attorney-General. That brought Colonel McCook hot-foot from West Virginia to Canton. He said: "I understood I was to be Attorney-General!" McKinley said: "Oh, no, colonel! You are to be Secretary of the Interior."

"I don't believe that place would suit me," replied McCook.

"Well," said McKinley, "we will try to find something equally good later on." McKinley thereby killed two birds with one stone; he avoided the religious issue and pleased Mark Hanna, who greatly disliked McCook.

McKinley tried to get Mark Hanna to accept the Postmaster-General's office, but he refused. He kept the place open for him until thirty-six hours before his inauguration. Urging Hanna to accept, he said: "Mark, you will feel pretty bad to see the ship of state sail away on the 4th of March and not be on board as first mate!"

At the last moment Mr. Gary, of Baltimore, was made Postmaster-General.

Two days after it was decided that Mr. Gage was to be the treasury chief, Frank A. Vanderlip came to see me. He was a reporter on *The Economist*, a Chicago financial weekly of a high order. I think he owned 20 per cent of the stock, and received a salary of $40 a week. He had been financial editor of the Chicago *Tribune*.

He asked me what I thought of his going to Washington with Mr. Gage as his private secretary. I answered: "Frank, you are too big a man to be anybody's private secretary!"

"The experience will benefit me greatly in my work on *The Economist*."

"Well," I answered, "you would be a good choice for Mr. Gage, as you can be of great service in handling the politicians and newspaper men."

Next morning Mr. Gage telephoned me to stop for him. He asked what I thought of his taking Vanderlip. I told him what I had told Vanderlip the day before.

Three months after going to Washington, Vanderlip was made an Assistant Secretary of the Treasury, at a salary of $4,500, more money than he ever received before in his life. He was of great assistance to Mr. Gage. They became intimate friends, and the friendship has lasted to this day.

When the National City Bank of New York purchased the old United States Custom House in Wall Street, Mr. Gage turned over to Vanderlip all the negotiations for the Treasury Department, which brought him in contact with the elder James Stillman frequently.   Mr. Stillman said to Mr. Gage: "When you are through with that young man, I want him."

Vanderlip finally went to the National City Bank, and Mr. Stillman told me afterward he showed him his desk, gave him the key to it and said: "Now find something to do.   Your salary will be $15,000 a year."

I have watched many notable careers in my time, but I think Frank Vanderlip's rise from a forty-dollars-a-week reporter in 1897 to the presidency of the greatest bank in the country in 1909 is the most remarkable of forty years' experience.

XIII

McKINLEY AND CLEVELAND

PRESIDENT MCKINLEY was inaugurated March 4, 1897. A few days later I took supper with Mrs. McKinley and him in the White House. Mrs. McKinley insisted it was supper and not dinner. The food was of the simplest kind, such as is served in thousands of homes in the Middle West. I noticed the colored butler waited on the President first. Mr. McKinley saw my look of surprise, and when the man left the room said: "That is one of the things I cannot get used to. All my married life Mrs. McKinley has been served first, but it is a custom and we cannot change it. We are governed by White House etiquette, handed down for generations. The employees pass from one administration to another. Some have been here over thirty years."

The President assisted Mrs. McKinley to the living-rooms above and rejoined me at the end of the hall, where palm-trees and rattan furniture gave an effect of summer. Neither of us spoke for ten or fifteen minutes. Finally McKinley, with a whimsical smile, said:

"What are you thinking about?"

"I was wondering if you would be wearing the same-sized hatband in a year from now."

"Do you think I am in danger of a swelled head?"

"You would be more than human if you were not influenced by the adulation paid you by 98 per cent of your callers.   Not more than 2 per cent tell you the truth!"

"Well, if you see evidence of an expansion, please tell me."

About a year later we were sitting in the same place, smoking.   McKinley said:

"Have you seen any evidences of my hatband expanding?"

"No," I answered, "but I am still watching it!"

The President told me that on returning from the inauguration exercises with ex-President Cleveland to the White House, Mr. Cleveland said: "I am deeply sorry, Mr. President, to pass on to you a war with Spain.   It will come within two years.   Nothing can stop it."

McKinley thought it could be avoided.   His pacific nature could not visualize war.   For the moment he was supremely happy.   Thirteen months later, April 21, 1898, Mr. Cleveland's prophecy came true.

The first sign of a break in the McKinley cabinet was when Secretary of State John Sherman gave evidence of mental deterioration.   His memory failed

SECRETARY OF STATE HAY

him on matters of vital importance, which embarrassed the President very much. When war with Spain was declared, McKinley felt he must have some one in the State Department on whom he could rely; so he wrote his old intimate friend Judge William R. Day, of Canton, and asked him to accept the position of Assistant Secretary of State. I was with the President when a telegram was handed him. He said: "It is from Judge Day, accepting the Assistant Secretary of State. He gives up $15,000 a year to take a $4,500 position. He would not do it if he did not love me." Judge Day's acceptance was a great relief to McKinley. Secretary Sherman soon retired and Judge Day became Secretary of State, until Ambassador John Hay came from London a few months later and assumed the office.

Colonel Hay told me it was a great disappointment to give up the ambassadorship. He loved the London life, but he added: "I am a soldier and go where I am sent."

XIV

THE SPANISH WAR

FEBRUARY 15, 1898, the *Maine* was blown up in Havana harbor. The event stirred the country against Spain. In April I received a wire from Secretary Cortelyou, as follows: "The President wants to see you."

At Harper's Ferry a telegram invited me to dine with the President and Mrs. McKinley. My train was two hours behind time, making it too late for dinner. So I wired that I would come as soon as possible.

There was a piano recital in the Blue Room of the White House. Mrs. McKinley was seated near the pianist, looking very frail and ill. The President was in the centre of the room on an S-shaped settee. There were eighteen or twenty guests present. As I stood in the doorway some one said: "The President is trying to catch your eye." He motioned me to sit by him, and whispered: "As soon as she is through this piece go and speak to Mrs. McKinley and then go to the Red Room door. I will join you." I did as requested, and when he had shaken hands with some of the late arrivals we went into the Red Room. We sat on a large crimson-brocade lounge. McKinley rested his head on his hands, with elbows on knees. He was in much distress, and said: "I have been through a trying period. Mrs. McKinley has been in poorer health than usual. It seems to me I have not slept over three hours a night for over two weeks. Congress is trying to drive us into war with Spain. The Spanish fleet is in Cuban waters, and we haven't enough ammunition on the Atlantic seacoast to fire a salute."

He broke down and cried like a boy of thirteen. I put my hand on his shoulder and remained silent, as I thought the tension would be relieved by his tears. As he became calm, I tried to assure him that the country would back him in any course he should pursue. He finally said:

"Are my eyes very red? Do they look as if I had been crying?"

"Yes."

"But I must return to Mrs. McKinley at once. She is among strangers."

"When you open the door to enter the room, blow your nose very hard and loud. It will force tears into your eyes and they will think that is what makes your eyes red." He acted on this suggestion and it was no small blast.

After the musicale the President and I went into the old cabinet room and talked until very late.

A few days afterward Congress voted to put

$50,000,000 in McKinley's hands—with no string on it.   War was declared April 21, 1898.

Ten days later, May 1, 1898, the battle of Manila was fought.   I visited the President a few days after the victory.   McKinley said: "When we received the cable from Admiral Dewey telling of the taking of the Philippines I looked up their location on the globe.   I could not have told where those darned islands were within 2,000 miles!"   Some months later he said: "If old Dewey had just sailed away when he smashed that Spanish fleet, what a lot of trouble he would have saved us."

The battle of Santiago was fought July 3, 1898, and saw the Spanish fleet sunk and the war ended.

McKinley told me they had Admiral Schley on the carpet to court-martial him for disobedience of orders in leaving Porto Rico and going to Santiago, but his successful fight against Cervera so completely captured the imagination of the people they dropped the proceedings, as they would have been resented by the country.

Poor Admiral Sampson never received the credit to which he was entitled for his part in the destruction of the Spanish fleet.   He died a disappointed man.

XV

THE PORTO RICO TARIFF

IN the Treaty of Peace with Spain signed at Paris, December 10, 1898, we acquired the Philippines, Porto Rico, and Guam, paying Spain $20,000,000 for them. She ceded the islands to us April 11, 1899.

The question of a tariff on imports from Porto Rico was the subject of much debate in the Senate in March, 1900. The Chicago *Times-Herald*, under my ownership, strongly opposed the 15 per cent tariff against our island territory, claiming it had the same rights as the territories Arizona and New Mexico. Senator Hanna made the fight against free imports from Porto Rico. I could not understand his opposition, and wrote and wired him there was great surprise and resentment that he should so oppose one of our new territories. He wrote me as follows:

UNITED STATES SENATE
WASHINGTON, D. C.

March 14, 1900

MY DEAR KOHLSAAT:

I do not agree with you on the Porto Rico Tariff Measure and I honestly believe if you had been here you would not have taken such a position, but as I have no idea that I can change your views, I will not enter into an argument. I feel my responsibilities and shall stand by our policy here, which I know is right.

Sincerely yours,

M. A. HANNA.

Some days later, in reply to a telegram from me, he wrote again:

UNITED STATES SENATE
WASHINGTON, D. C

March 27th, 1900

MY DEAR KOHLSAAT:

I am in receipt of your telegram and reply that I am sorry the people are so very sore over my "implied defiance," and yet it is strange that every one who comes here and gets to know the facts and politics of the thing goes away satisfied I am doing all I can to bring about a solution of the trouble, while you fellows are doing all you can to prevent it. Time will tell who is right and I have no excuses to offer for my course. Of course I am the one to blame and have been for four years, but my time is nearly up and you can soon choose a new "buffer" for all party discussions. I have not been out of touch with my party here and am not worrying over my fate, but when you hear of my recognizing Porto Rico as an integral part of the United States and all that goes with it, you can make up your mind I am as crazy as Beveridge. Now let me give you some good advice: Drop the agitation and give us a chance to settle the matter in Congress and then you can give me all the Hell you want to; to do it now is no good.

Sincerely yours,

M. A. HANNA.

The Foraker Act, making Porto Rico imports free after March 2, 1902, went into effect April 3, 1900.

After the passage of the Foraker Bill I asked Senator Hanna to tell me frankly why he took the position he did. He laughed and said: "I'll tell you exactly. We received notice from 250,000 Union cigar-rollers that if we admitted Porto Rico cigars free of duty, each of the 250,000 would get three other Union men to vote against the Republican party in November, 1900, making 1,000,000 votes against McKinley."

XVI

THE OPEN DOOR IN CHINA

In 1900 President McKinley and Secretary of State Hay approached the Powers, demanding the "open door" and equal opportunity in China.

Before announcing his Far East policy, McKinley unfolded his plans to me. His great ambition was to create new markets for American producers and manufacturers. He wanted to keep our people busy. His motto was: "Regular employment, good wages, and education bring prosperity and happiness."

Colonel John Hay, as our ambassador in London, met the ambassadors and statesmen of the world. He was exceedingly popular with them, which greatly aided his efforts to bring them and their governments to an agreement on the "open door."

I spent some hours with him in his library, and promised to aid in creating sentiment among the people of the Northwest to urge their senators and representatives to back McKinley and Hay in their Chinese negotiations.

The treaties were ratified, and have been the means of creating new markets for our goods and bringing about a better understanding between the Far East and the United States.

Newbury, N.H.

DEPARTMENT OF STATE.
WASHINGTON

Aug. 11, '00

Dear Mr. Hollisack.

I have received your kind letter of Feb. 7th and the enclosed leader from the Iowa-Herald. I was not as here much I am obliged to you. Some very thoughtfully sent me a marked copy of Stilson Hutchins paper which said I was going of severe and stern

in their thoughfulness and that they were so — glad of it, and that it seemed to be a good for the country if I had been any go. I have things are said with each

several remarks and leaving that I everything unsaid if they are not true. But when I see what a judicious press can you say, I feel as if I had the right thing on a while.

Give my compliments to Mrs. Hollisack and believe me always

Sincerely yours
John Hay

The following letters were among those received during the "open door" negotiations:

DEPARTMENT OF STATE

WASHINGTON

March 30, 1900.

My dear Mr. Kohlsaat:

Allow me to thank you most sincerely for your editorial approval of our Chinese negotiations. Your strong and well-weighed words, and Wellman's articles will put the matter in its true light before the great North Western public. Your action is most valuable to us all and I am cordially grateful to you for it.

Yours faithfully,

John Hay.

Newbury, N. H., Aug. 11, '00.

Dear Mr. Kohlsaat:

I have received your kind letter of the 7th and the inclosed leader from *The Times-Herald*. I need not say how much I am obliged to you. Somebody thoughtfully sent me a marked copy of Stilson Hutchins' paper which said I was dying of remorse and shame in New Hampshire and that they were d—— glad of it, and that it would be a good job for the country if I had died long ago. These things are said with such evident earnestness and sincerity that I sometimes wonder if they are not true. But when I see what a judicious person like you says, I feel as if I had the right to live on a while.

Give my compliments to Mrs. Kohlsaat and believe me always

Sincerely yours

John Hay.

XVII

THE HAY–PAUNCEFOTE TREATY

THE Hay-Pauncefote treaty negotiations began in 1900, and were finally closed in 1901.

The first treaty was defeated in the Senate because a majority of the senators strongly objected to the non-fortification feature. They did not believe the world had advanced far enough toward universal peace to permit leaving the canal unprotected.

Their fears were justified in the World War of 1914 to 1918, when the news was received that a German raider was sinking ships in the south Atlantic. What would have happened to the Panama Canal if it had not been fortified?

After the Senate defeat, Messrs. Hay and Pauncefote amended the treaty authorizing fortifications, and resubmitted it to the Senate. It was ratified with little delay.

Lord Pauncefote, the British ambassador, died in Washington the next year, May 26, 1902. He was greatly respected for his personal charm and statesmanship.

I was in the old cabinet room with President Roosevelt one noon in June, 1902, when his barber brought in a skeleton reclining-chair. Taking off his coat, but not his collar, the President reclined on the chair. The barber lathered his face and began shaving him, but Roosevelt did not stop talking. I said: "He will cut you if you don't stop making faces and talking." The look the knight of the razor gave me for even suggesting such a thing silenced me.

Major Loeffler, an appointee of President Grant's who had guarded the President's door ever since, announced "Secretary of State Hay and Mr. Raikes of the British Embassy." Roosevelt said: "Show them into the library, major; I'll see them in a few minutes."

Without turning his face he said: "I know what they want. John Hay has brought Raikes to thank me for putting the flag at half-mast on the White House when old Pauncefote died. I didn't do it because he was the British ambassador, but because he was a damn good fellow."

XVIII

ROOSEVELT AND HIS ROUGH RIDERS

In June, 1899, Paul Morton, at that time vice-president of the Santa Fé Railroad, telephoned me he had offered his private car to Governor Roosevelt, of New York, to go to the Rough Riders' Reunion at Las Vegas, N. M. Roosevelt accepted Morton's offer, and asked him to invite me to go with them.

Up to this time neither Morton nor I had met Governor Roosevelt. We left Chicago at 6 o'clock one evening and sat up very late to hear the colonel tell his Cuban war experiences. Next morning at 7 o'clock we arrived in Kansas City. A few train-hands recognized Roosevelt and shook hands with him. A short time after crossing the river we stopped at a water-tank in Kansas. It was a wonderful June morning. Roosevelt was abounding in good spirits. A wizen-faced old woman in a faded sunbonnet was the only human being in sight. She came out of a tumble-down shack, walked up the track, and looked at Roosevelt. He gave her a hearty "good morning." She made no reply, but came to the car and held up a hand like a sparrow's claw and said: "Shake, Teddy." Roosevelt took the proffered hand just as the train started. He cocked his head one side and watched the old sun-bonnet until we passed out of sight.   With a queer twist of his mouth he said: "I suppose that is meant as a token of affection, but even my wife calls me 'Theodore.'"

Morton had wired the Santa Fé agents Roosevelt was on the train, and at every stop crowds gathered around the car to shake hands and hear him speak. He made the same speech at each town.   In several of the larger cities the men had printed cards stuck in their hatbands which read: "Roosevelt in 1904."

At Emporia, Kans., the home of William Allen White, a brass band escorted Roosevelt to a speaker's stand a few hundred yards from the train.   I am not sure, but I think it was the first meeting of Roose-velt and White.

The night we left Emporia, Roosevelt, Morton, and I talked until midnight.   Roosevelt was puzzled over the "Roosevelt 1904" cards.   I told him the people were going to give McKinley a second term in 1900, and he, Roosevelt, was evidently their choice for 1904.

In speaking of President McKinley he said: "Mc-Kinley has a chocolate-éclair backbone."   I told him he was mistaken, and then related how he had prac-tically thrown away the chance of the Presidential nomination in 1896 when he declined to promise Tom Platt the Secretary of the Treasury post in return for the vote of New York and Pennsylvania. (This story I have told in describing Mark Hanna's visit to Platt and Quay in an earlier chapter.) Roosevelt said: "By George, is that so! I take back my remark about his backbone!"

I then told him of my years of friendship with McKinley—that he had not made a speech outside of Ohio for seven years without either wiring, telephoning, or writing me, and sending me his speeches to read before delivering them.

Next morning at breakfast I apologized for seeming boastfulness and asked him not to lay it up against me. He said: "Do you know what I thought after I went to bed? I wondered if you would do the same thing for me."

The telegrams and letters that follow show our subsequent relations.

The next day a delegation of Colorado men joined our party in their own sleepers and went to Las Vegas.

When we arrived in the famous New Mexican town a great crowd met us at the station. There were a number of real live cowboys in the crowd. They yelled and waved their hats when Roosevelt appeared, and shot off their revolvers. The town was alive day and night the three days we spent there. Everything was wide open. No pen can describe Roosevelt's enthusiasm. He bubbled over every

The White Nile
March 12th 1910

My dear fellow,

By George,
It is fine to have you
again at the head of
a great newspaper
But, oh how I wish you
and your paper were
in New York!

I was mighty glad
to see Wellman and
get your note. I
hope to see you as
soon as possible after
I get back to
America,

Ever yours
Theodore Roosevelt

H. H. Kohlsaat
Record Herald
Chicago Ill
U. S. A.

minute. Our car was filled with Rough Riders, who told lurid stories of experiences in Cuba. One of the cowboys, with a big scar on his face, said: "Colonel, do you remember the night it rained hell and wild-cats?" "By George, wasn't that a bully storm"—and the white teeth snapped.

We left Las Vegas amid the same sort of demonstration as on our arrival. Roosevelt stood on the back platform and waved his cowboy sombrero until the foot-hills shut off the view of the town.

One of the Colorado delegates, a high state official, came into Morton's car and said to me: "I want to apologize to you." "What for?" "Well, you put the word 'gold' into the Republican platform in '96. That gave Colorado the worst blow she ever had. We faced ruin. If you had come to Denver or any other Colorado city at that time, you would have been mobbed. We have been together for four days, and I want to apologize for the hatred I bore you."

The return to Chicago was quieter than the going West. At night we discussed national and industrial affairs. Roosevelt was very much interested in Paul Morton's views of the railroad situation, and the legislation necessary to carry out the reforms he suggested. They were later put into effect when Roosevelt became President. He offered Morton the post of Secretary of the Navy in 1904. Morton at first declined the position, with the remark: "The only ship I know anything about is the prairie-schooner!" Roosevelt said: "Don't worry about that. I know all about ships. What I want of you is your railroad knowledge!"

From Chicago Roosevelt went to Milwaukee to deliver a speech. Next day I joined him and went to New York. We arrived in La Porte, Ind., as Roosevelt was ready for bed. There were about a thousand people at the station calling for him. He did not hear them until I opened his stateroom door. Hastily pulling on his trousers over his pajamas, he rushed to the rear platform as the train started, and yelled: "Good night and good luck!"

Early next morning we arrived in Buffalo. There was no cheering crowd to welcome him; with the exception of the train-crew, the only person in sight was the chap who hits the coach-wheels with a hammer.

I said: "Governor, you are at home." He answered: "Yes, by George, they know me here!"

During the day I suggested that he send a telegram to President McKinley telling of the sentiment he had found in the West for his renomination in 1900, and the proffer of his personal support. I wired the Associated Press correspondent to please meet the train at Albany. Roosevelt gave him an interview and read him his message to McKinley.

A few days later I received a wire from him saying he had received a telegram from the President to bring Mrs. Roosevelt and spend Sunday at the White House. I append subsequent letters from him received during the next three months.

STATE OF NEW YORK
EXECUTIVE CHAMBER
ALBANY

July 1, 1899

MY DEAR MR. KOHLSAAT:

Was my McKinley interview all right?

Remember me warmly to Mrs. Kohlsaat.

Incidentally, permit me to remark that you are a trump and no mistake! Didn't we have a good week together?

Faithfully yours,

THEODORE ROOSEVELT.

STATE OF NEW YORK
EXECUTIVE CHAMBER
ALBANY

At Oyster Bay, N. Y., July 5th, 1899

MY DEAR MR. KOHLSAAT:

I thank you for yours of the 2nd inst. and was greatly interested in the clipping you sent me. I am delighted that you like my interview. I cannot say how I enjoyed meeting you, and indeed, our whole trip. I am now receiving numerous invitations to go west at different times. I shall consult you before accepting any. It hardly seems necessary to go out this summer or fall again. Does it to you?

Again heartily thanking you, I am

Faithfully yours,

THEODORE ROOSEVELT.

STATE OF NEW YORK
EXECUTIVE CHAMBER
ALBANY

At Oyster Bay, N. Y., Aug. 7th, 1899.

MY DEAR MR. KOHLSAAT:

I write you for two bits of advice.

1. The Minnesota League of Republican Clubs want me to come out there on November 1st. I do not feel much like going at this time. I do not see that the good that I could do would counterbalance the strain and effort, and think I had better keep my western trip for some future time. What do you think?

2. How about trusts? I know this is a very large question, but more and more it seems to me that there will be a good deal of importance to the trust matter in the next campaign and I want to consult with men whom I trust as to what line of policy should be pursued. During the last few months I have been growing exceedingly alarmed at the growth of popular unrest and popular distrust on this question. It is largely aimless and baseless, but there is a very unpleasant side to this overrun trust development and what I fear is if we do not have some consistent policy to advocate then the multitudes will follow the crank who advocates an absurd policy, but who does advocate something. Have you thought enough about the matter to say whether any legislation, and if so, what should be undertaken? Or, whether there is any other remedy that can be wisely applied.

Faithfully yours,
THEODORE ROOSEVELT.

Telegram

Oyster Bay, Aug. 11, 1899

H. H. Kohlsaat,
 Times-Herald,
  Chicago.

Ohio people want me to open campaign. Seems to me I ought to go so as to make one western speech, and that McKinley's own state. What do you think? Please wire reply.

THEODORE ROOSEVELT.

STATE OF NEW YORK
EXECUTIVE CHAMBER
ALBANY

At Oyster Bay, Aug. 12, 1899

MY DEAR MR. KOHLSAAT:

I acted promptly on your telegram about the Ohio campaign.

Now, oh mentor! Will you advise me about the enclosed? I hardly think of accepting. I think I had better wait until Galena Day.

Faithfully yours,
THEODORE ROOSEVELT.

Telegram

Utica, N. Y. September 13, '99.

H. H. Kohlsaat,
 Times-Herald,
  Chicago.

Henderson and Allison want me to open campaign in Iowa at Waterloo October 7th. Very difficult for me to go. Ought I to accept?

THEODORE ROOSEVELT.

STATE OF NEW YORK
EXECUTIVE CHAMBER
ALBANY

August 20th, 1899

MY DEAR MR. KOHLSAAT:

I thank you for yours of the 14th inst. Your advice is as sound as a dollar, a good deal sounder than a forty-eight cent dollar. When the President requested me to go to Ohio of course I had to go. That is all I shall do. I have, however, consented to give the gold medal to the returning 10th Regiment of Pennsylvania Troops, because that was something that seemed appropriate and proper. However, it is not yet definitely determined that I shall go there.

Faithfully yours,

THEODORE ROOSEVELT.

STATE OF NEW YORK
EXECUTIVE CHAMBER
ALBANY

At Oyster Bay, September 19, 1899.

MY DEAR MR. KOHLSAAT:

Just a line of thanks for your telegram. I have declined the Iowa invitation. You have been the most successful mentor, though I should think you would be tired of the job by this time. I will keep faith that you are going to be on here to visit me, if possible with Mrs. Kohlsaat. We should so like to have you both, either here or at Albany.

Faithfully yours,

THEODORE ROOSEVELT.

XIX

ROOSEVELT AND THE VICE–PRESIDENCY

THE telegram Governor Roosevelt sent President McKinley the end of June, 1899, pledging his support to McKinley for renomination in 1900, which led to an invitation to bring Mrs. Roosevelt and spend Sunday at the White House, brought about a great change in McKinley's feelings toward Roosevelt.

Some of Roosevelt's friends had irritated McKinley and Hanna in bringing him forward as a candidate against McKinley for the Presidential nomination in 1900. When Roosevelt pledged his support, all opposition for renomination disappeared. McKinley had the field to himself.

There was a strong demand for Roosevelt, especially in the West, for Vice-President, on the ticket with McKinley. His spectacular career as colonel of the Rough Riders endeared him to the young men of the country.

Senator Platt wanted to get Roosevelt out of the governor's office in New York, and seized the opportunity offered by the boom for him as Vice-President to realize his hopes.

Roosevelt and most of his friends fought the effort to shove him into the Vice-Presidency.

In February, 1900, I wrote him strongly advising him not to be a candidate. His reply was as follows:

EXECUTIVE CHAMBER
ALBANY

February 9, 1900

MY DEAR MR. KOHLSAAT:

I thank you heartily for yours of the 8th inst. with enclosed clipping. The Vice Presidency was one of the few things I made up my mind it was not needful to write you about. I am not going to take it on any account. Mr. Payne of Milwaukee and Senator Lodge, as well, are anxious that I should, but it is the very last office I would want or care for. In two or three days I shall announce this publicly.

Faithfully yours,

THEODORE ROOSEVELT.

March 21st I received the following telegram:

Can you not stop off here to take lunch or spend the night? Very anxious to see you.

THEODORE ROOSEVELT.

We were together several hours and thoroughly discussed the Vice-Presidency and some tax matters which were disturbing Senator Platt and the banking interests in New York City.

June 16th he wrote me the following letter, in part:

EXECUTIVE CHAMBER

ALBANY

June 16, 1900

MY DEAR MR. KOHLSAAT:

I shall have to face a rough fight here next fall, because the lunatic Goo Goo, the wealthy corporation corruptionist and the basest variety of machine politician will all join my ordinary party foes in trying to beat me. But I have never hesitated in my belief that it was far better to chance such a fight and go down than to take an office for which I really had no special fitness and where there was nothing for a man of my type to do.

Hastily, but always faithfully yours,

THEODORE ROOSEVELT.

A few days later the Republican national convention was held in Philadelphia. I did not attend, but sent him a wire urging him not to take the Vice-Presidential nomination. He received it during the session, and sent word he would not accept under any circumstances.

Mark Hanna was bitterly against his nomination, but McKinley was inclined to favor him.

George W. Perkins, of New York, told me he telephoned McKinley strongly advocating Roosevelt's nomination. He said he thought he influenced McKinley to telephone Mr. Hanna to throw his strength to Roosevelt, as he believed his nomination would strengthen the ticket.

Mr. Hanna favored Senator Dolliver, of Iowa, John D. Long, of Massachusetts, Secretary of the

Navy, or anybody, rather than Roosevelt.   He later
told B. B. Odell, of New York, he would have thrown
his influence to him if New York had wanted the
Vice-Presidency.   Mr. Odell declined, and threw
away the chance to be President!

Two or three years later Nicholas Murray Butler
told me the following story:

Frederick Holls and I had been out for a walk with
T. R., during which he had insisted with all the emphasis
at his command that never, no, never, would he be brow-
beaten by Platt and Quay into accepting the nomination
for Vice President!   When we got back to the Hotel Wal-
ton we stood at the bottom of the elevator shaft, and
after waiting several minutes were told that the elevator
was out of commission for a bit, and that we must either
wait or walk up stairs to our rooms on the seventh floor.
While we were waiting Lemuel Ely Quigg and Frank H.
Platt joined us and after taking Roosevelt aside for a
few minutes walked him up with them to a room on the
mezzanine floor.   There he talked with Senator Platt
personally.   An hour later T. R. rejoined us in our headquarters; his tail feathers were all down.   The fight had
gone out of him and he changed his former tune to that
of "I cannot disappoint my western friends, if they insist,
etc.   I cannot seem to be bigger than the party, etc."
The deed had been done and the rest you know!

The face of history might have been changed if
that elevator had not gone out of commission!

McKinley and Roosevelt were nominated and
elected, defeating William Jennings Bryan for the

second time by a vote of 7,219,530 to 6,358,074, a plurality of 861,459.

When McKinley and Roosevelt were inaugurated March 4, 1901, some one asked Senator Platt if he was going to attend the inaugural exercises. He replied: "Yes, I am going to Washington to see Theodore Roosevelt take the veil!"

XX

ROOSEVELT AND THE PRIZE–FIGHT

SATURDAY, August 30, 1901, Vice-President Roosevelt was in Chicago on his way to Minnesota to deliver a speech at the State Fair.

I invited a few friends to meet him at dinner in the Chicago Club. As I left him in his hotel room he said he would like to attend service in a Dutch Reformed Church Sunday morning. I called for him and took him to a small, unfinished brick church on the West Side. When we got into the carriage he pulled a pink sheet out of his breast-pocket and said: "There was a prize-fight last week. I did not want to attract attention by reading it at the breakfast-table in the hotel!" He had not finished it when we reached the church, and so put it in his pocket!

We arrived while the minister, Doctor Moerdyke, was praying. The usher looked critically at Roosevelt, as if he could hardly believe it really was the Vice-President attending services in their little church, which held probably 150 people. When the prayer ended, I introduced him to Roosevelt. We were shown into the front pew. During the singing of a hymn the usher stepped up to the pastor, and probably assured him it really was the Vice-President!

Roosevelt sang louder than any one in the congregation and made the responses in a vigorous voice. Doctor Moerdyke's text was: "Be ye doers of the word and not hearers only."

At the close of the sermon the pastor said: "We are honored by having with us to-day a fellow member of our church, the Vice-President of the United States, Theodore Roosevelt. I am going to ask him to speak to us." Before he had finished, Roosevelt literally sprang out of his seat and mounted to the pulpit and began to talk on the text of the morning.

He threw his fists right and left—uppercuts and undercuts. Evidently his subconscious mind was dwelling on the prize-fight! He ran to the farther side of the pulpit and struck out with so much vehemence that he terrified a child two or three years of age, eight or ten feet away. It screamed, and not only startled the congregation but embarrassed the poor mother. She picked the youngster up and started out of the church. Roosevelt said: "Sit down, please, madam. Don't go out. I have six of them of my own at home, and am used to crying children!" The woman took her seat, but the child continued to yell, and finally compelled Roosevelt to stop talking. He left the pulpit and shook hands with each person present.

When we left the church quite a crowd outside cheered him as we drove away. A block or two from the church he pulled the pink sheet out of his pocket and resumed the story of the fight, remarking: "By George, that was a bully fight. Sorry I missed it!"

XXI

PRESIDENT McKINLEY'S ASSASSINATION

PRESIDENT McKINLEY and Mrs. McKinley visited the Buffalo Fair in September, 1901. On the 5th the President delivered a memorable address in the Fair Grounds. He called for a greater participation in world affairs and putting an end to isolation.

He held a reception in the Temple of Music—one of the Fair buildings—on September 6, and shook hands with hundreds of men, women, and children. A man approached with a handkerchief covering his hand. As the President held out his hand, a shot startled the crowd. Under the handkerchief was a pistol. McKinley was shot in the arm and stomach. The Secret Service men grasped the lunatic, Leon Czolgosz, and were treating him roughly. When McKinley saw it, he asked them not to hurt him.

After examination the President was taken to the home of John G. Milburn, president of the Buffalo Fair. For several days it seemed as if he had a chance to recover, as the following telegrams would indicate:

Buffalo, September 8, 1901.

H. H. KOHLSAAT,
  Chicago.

I wish to contradict false despatches that I predicted the President would not live. His condition this morning greatly improved. If this continues a day or two we may hope for speedy recovery.

M. A. HANNA.

Buffalo, September 9, 1901

H. H. KOHLSAAT,
   Chicago.

All now firm in belief that the President will speedily recover.

MYRON T. HERRICK.

Secretary Cortelyou wired me the doctors' bulletins daily. The last two telegrams received from him were as follows:

Buffalo, September 14, 1901
1:40, A. M.

H. H. KOHLSAAT,
   Chicago.

The President is dying.

GEORGE B. CORTELYOU.

Buffalo, September 14, 1901
4:34 A. M.

H. H. KOHLSAAT,
   Chicago.

The President passed away at a quarter after two o'clock this morning.

GEORGE B. CORTELYOU.

If the President's physical condition had been good he might have survived his wounds, but the doctors said, after his death, they doubted if he would have lived two years, as several organs were badly diseased.

McKinley made a brave fight, but became weaker daily, and passed away early Saturday morning. In semiconscious moments he repeated several times:

"Nearer, my God, to Thee, nearer to Thee." Once he had said to me: "If it was not for Ida [his wife], I should like to go the way Lincoln did." He had his wish.

I left Chicago Saturday night, arriving in Buffalo Sunday morning, and telephoned Senator Hanna, who was a guest of his friends the Hamlins.

I asked him how to get into the Milburn residence for the funeral exercises, as the house was surrounded by militia. He asked me to go with him. We went in the rear gate and entered the house through the kitchen, where I took a seat until Secretary Cortelyou took me into the small library where the casket was placed.

Among the few men in the library when I entered was Charles G. Dawes, whose grief could not have been greater had his own father been in the coffin.

President Roosevelt, who had been sworn in the day before, came in with six out of eight members of his cabinet. They were Elihu Root, Secretary of War; Ethan A. Hitchcock, Secretary of the Interior; John D. Long, Secretary of the Navy; James L. Wilson, Secretary of Agriculture; Charles Emory Smith, Postmaster-General; Philander C. Knox, Attorney-General. The other members of the cabinet, John Hay, Secretary of State, and Lyman J. Gage, Secretary of the Treasury, were in Washington.

As the President and his cabinet seated them-

selves beside the casket, poor, broken-hearted Mark
Hanna limped in and took a chair at the foot of the
coffin.   For a while he rested his head on his hand,
with elbows on knees.   Finally he sat up straight
and, with folded arms, put on a brave face.

There is an impression that Mark Hanna controlled William McKinley.   That is not so.   His attitude was always that of a big, bashful boy toward
a girl he loves.   It was not the power that it brought
Mr. Hanna that made him fight for McKinley's
nomination and election; it was the love of a strong
man for a friend who was worthy of that affection.

Before the services began President Roosevelt came
to me and said: "Come to Ansley Wilcox's house on
Delaware Avenue at 3 o'clock.   I want to see you."

After the services in the Milburn residence the
casket was taken to the City Hall, where thousands
passed the bier before midnight.

At 3 o'clock I gave my card to the colored man at
the Wilcox home.   The house was old-fashioned.   A
hall with rooms on both sides.   My card was carried
into the room on the right.   Across the hall were
the members of the cabinet.   I was soon shown in;
after I had shaken hands with Roosevelt, he turned
to a gentleman by his side and said: "Woodrow,
you know Kohlsaat, don't you?   Mr. Kohlsaat, let
me introduce you to Woodrow Wilson."

After a moment or two Roosevelt said: "Woodrow, would you mind stepping into the library for a few minutes? I want to talk to Kohlsaat on an important matter." In 1901 Mr. Wilson was professor of political economy and jurisprudence, Princeton University. A year later he was made president of the institution.

After Mr. Wilson left us, Roosevelt said: "I am going to make two changes in my cabinet that I know will please you. I am going to let John Hay go and appoint Elihu Root Secretary of State. I am also going to ask Lyman Gage for his resignation." I answered: "Why do you think it would please me to have Hay go?" He said: "Why, Hay's position on the Hay-Pauncefote treaty was what brought you and me together." I said: "John Hay is a warm friend of mine. Instead of sulking when the treaty was defeated, he was man enough to amend it to allow fortifications, and it was finally ratified. And," I continued, "what have you against Lyman Gage?" Roosevelt snapped his teeth and said: "He always gets his back up against the wall, and I can't get around him." I said: "Don't you know I am responsible for Mr. Gage being in the cabinet? McKinley did not know him. He appointed him inside of five minutes, after a long-distance telephone from Chicago to Canton, in January, 1897."

I continued: "Yesterday, when you were sworn in, you issued a statement that you were going to carry on McKinley's policies, and now you propose to fire his Secretary of State and Secretary of the Treasury! Saturday the stock exchanges of the country closed when the news came of McKinley's death. To-day's papers report there is great uneasiness as to what will happen when they open to-morrow. Why? Because you are considered a 'bucking bronco' in finance, and now you propose to let Gage out of the Treasury Department, and Heaven only knows whom you will appoint. It will probably cause a panic, and it will be known for all time as the 'Roosevelt panic.'"

Roosevelt looked at me a moment, made one of his characteristic faces, and in one of those falsetto notes of his said: "Old man, I am going to pay you the highest compliment I ever paid any one in my life. I am going to keep both of them!"

He then insisted I go to Washington with him on the funeral train at 8.30 the next morning. I told him it was impossible, as I had to be in Chicago Monday morning to borrow $10,000 for my *Record-Herald* pay-roll. He said: "Do you remember what you said to me a few minutes ago?—'You must!' Well, you 'must' go with me to-morrow. The only friend I have on the train is Elihu Root. If I talk to him all the time it will make the other fellows mad. Telephone your banker that I say you must go to Washington, and to take care of your pay-roll." That night I telephoned Ernest A. Hamill, president Corn Exchange National Bank, and was told to go ahead. "I will take care of your pay-roll."

Roosevelt continued to talk of his cabinet. He said: "Gage does not like me. I want you to wire him to meet you at your hotel on our arrival and tell him he must stay for a while, at least, and I want you to see the Associated Press man and ask him to send a despatch that when we reach Washington to-morrow night I am going to ask Hay and Gage to remain in the cabinet."

In 1904, during the Republican convention in Chicago, I met Secretary of Agriculture Wilson at the Chicago Club. He said: "What did you say to Roosevelt the day of the McKinley funeral in Buffalo at that house where we stopped?" I said: "Why, Uncle Jimmie?" "Well," he said, "when Roosevelt went to the door and you went down the steps, he rushed into the room where we six cabinet fellows were and said: 'I have changed my mind. I am going to keep all of you!' He had asked us for our resignations that morning, which, of course, is customary!"

Monday morning at 8.30 the funeral train left Buffalo. The President and cabinet preceded the casket to the special train, Mrs. McKinley, her friends, and George B. Cortelyou following. When the casket had been placed in the private car of some railroad official, President Roosevelt stepped up to me and said: "Did you send that telegram to Gage?" The newspaper men were very curious to know what Roosevelt whispered, and sent some wild conjectures to their papers.

The railroad officials had entirely cleared the depot of all cars, both sides of the track. Not a soul was to be seen on either platform, with the exception of the crew of the funeral train. In the thirteen hours it took to go to Washington, no cars of any sort were on the track next to our train. The railroad arrangements were perfect. The train consisted of a baggage, dining-car, three Pullman sleepers, and a private car. One coach was occupied by the President and cabinet; another by friends, including Senator Hanna, Charles G. Dawes, Charles W. Fairbanks, Cornelius N. Bliss, John G. Milburn, and Elmer Dover, secretary to Senator Hanna; the third by newspaper correspondents.

Roosevelt occupied a drawing-room. He asked me to sit with him. His mind was working like a trip-hammer. He talked of many things he was going to do.

Part of the time I was in the second Pullman. An hour or two after leaving Buffalo Mark Hanna came to my seat. He was in an intensely bitter state of mind. He damned Roosevelt and said: "I told William McKinley it was a mistake to nominate that wild man at Philadelphia. I asked him if he realized what would happen if he should die. Now look, that damned cowboy is President of the United States!"

I tried to reason with him; told him Roosevelt did not want to be "shot into the Presidency," but could not mollify him.

A little later I asked Roosevelt how he and Mark Hanna got along. He said: "Hanna treats me like a boy. He calls me 'Teddy.'" I asked him if he realized what it meant if he and Hanna quarrelled, and told him Hanna held the Republican organization in the hollow of his hand; that he was the leader in the Senate and could defeat any measure that he, Roosevelt, proposed, and make his administration a failure. I cited the Garfield-Conkling row.

Roosevelt said: "What can I do about it? Give him complete control of the patronage!" I said: "Hanna would resent any such suggestion." I told him Hanna was heart-broken. He saw his best friend gone. All his hopes crushed.

Finally I made the suggestion he invite Hanna to take supper with him alone in his drawing-room. That he must not say anything in the presence of the waiter that could be repeated, as the newspaper men would pounce upon the poor colored boy when they arrived in Washington. That after the plates and cloth were removed, to let the table remain, calling his attention to the awful gap between the front and back seat of a Pullman sleeper. When they were alone, to say: "'Old man, I want you to be my friend. I know you cannot give me the love and affection you gave McKinley, but I want you to give me just as much as you can. I need you. Will you be my friend?' Then put your hands, palms up, on the table. If he puts his hands in his pockets, you are a goner, but if he puts his hands in yours, you can bet on him for life." Roosevelt said: "All right, I'll try it!"

Later, as I sat in the forward coach, I saw the waiter whisper in Senator Hanna's ear. He hesitated a moment, and then nodded his head. He came to my seat at the other end of the car and said: "That damned cowboy wants me to take supper with him, alone. Damn him!" I said: "Mark, you are acting like a child. Go and meet him half-way."

Shortly after, he disappeared into Roosevelt's car. I was very nervous, but as an hour passed and thirty minutes more, Hanna came in, and I knew by his face, as he limped toward my seat, it was "all right." With a smile which the late Volney Foster said "would grease a wagon," Hanna said: "He's a pretty good little cuss, after all!" When I asked him what took place, he told me of Roosevelt's putting his hands on the table, and as near as one man can quote another, he told what Roosevelt said, repeating what I had told Roosevelt to say. "What did you do, Mark?" He answered: "Putting my hands in his I said: 'I will be your friend on two conditions: first, that you carry out McKinley's policies, as you promised.' Roosevelt answered: 'All right, I will.' 'Second, that you quit calling me "old man." If you don't, I'll call you "Teddy."' 'All right. You call me "Teddy" and I'll call you "old man."'" From that moment Roosevelt and Hanna were stanch, loyal friends. The only rift was for a few weeks late in 1903, when some anti-Roosevelt people tried to get Mark Hanna into the race for the Presidency.

All of Roosevelt's own writings and his numerous biographers tell of his friendly relations with Hanna, but are silent as to how it came about.

As the funeral train left Buffalo, the streets through which it passed were filled with men with bared heads, women, and children. As we went through the towns and cities, the station platforms were crowded with school-children, singing: "Nearer, my God, to Thee, nearer to Thee." The day was bright and warm for September. The windows of the car were up. As we neared the stations the engineer slacked speed and slowly passed the singing, weeping crowds. Before the day was over every one on the train was in a highly strained condition. Tears came easily.   It was an exhausted party that reached Washington at 9 o'clock that night.

For days after that trip, awake or asleep, I heard that "Near-urr, my God, to Thee, near-urr to Thee"!

At Harrisburg thousands of people in the depot shed were singing McKinley's last words.

As we neared Washington darkness came on; the negroes in Maryland lighted fires near the track. As the train passed we could see their dark forms and faces in the glare of the burning brushwood. Here, too, their song was: "Nearer, my God, to Thee, nearer to Thee."

During the entire day, in the last coach a little, frail figure in black kept tender watch over her beloved dead.

XXII

ROOSEVELT, HAY, AND GAGE

THE following telegram was received as the train halted at Harrisburg:

Washington, D. C.   September 16, 1901.
H. H. KOHLSAAT,
   Care Funeral Train,
      Harrisburg, Penna.
   Will come to Arlington Hotel to see you as soon as I can after your arrival.

LYMAN J. GAGE.

I bought the evening papers in Harrisburg, and read to Roosevelt a despatch from New York stating that his announcement made through the Associated Press that he would retain Hay and Gage in his cabinet had had a good effect in Wall Street.

"I don't care a damn about stocks and bonds," said Roosevelt, "but I don't want to see them go down the first day I am President!"

Secretaries Hay and Gage met us at the depot and rode with Roosevelt to the White House.   Later in the evening Mr. Gage came to the Arlington Hotel, and told me he had promised Roosevelt to remain for a while.   Four months later he resigned, and was succeeded by Leslie M. Shaw, of Iowa.

That Secretary of State Hay was uncertain whether he would remain in the cabinet is shown by the following letter in William Roscoe Thayer's admirable "Life of Hay," written to his intimate friend Henry Adams, September 19. 1901:

I have just received your letter from Stockholm and shudder at the awful clairvoyance of your last phrase about Teddy's luck.

Well, he is here in the saddle again. That is, he is in Canton to attend President McKinley's funeral, and will have his first Cabinet meeting in the White House tomorrow. He came down from Buffalo Monday night and in the station, without waiting an instant, told me I must stay with him, that I could not decline or even consider. I saw, of course, it was best for me to start off that way, and so I said I would stay, forever, of course, for it would be worse to say I would stay awhile, than it would be to go out at once. I can still go at any moment he gets tired of me, or when I collapse.

John Hay remained as Secretary of State in Roosevelt's cabinet until his death, July 1, 1905.

Elihu Root succeeded him July 6, 1905.

XXIII

ROOSEVELT AND GENERAL MILES

In the early summer of 1902 the papers announced
that President Roosevelt was going to remove General Nelson A. Miles as Lieutenant-General Commander of the army. I wrote him if the report was
true he would make a great mistake—that General
Miles, a volunteer himself, was the idol of the volunteer soldier of the Civil War. The veterans believed he was the victim of a West Point clique.
Two days later I received a telegram asking me to
come to Washington to talk over the Miles matter.

On my arrival at the White House President
Roosevelt was starting out for a horseback ride. He
at once plunged into the subject, but I told him to
take his ride, and I would see him later. He invited
me to dine with the family.

After dinner we went into the old cabinet room.
He showed me the papers of dismissal he was going
to hand General Miles Monday morning.

I again warned him he would make a mistake;
that I knew General Miles's irritating qualities, as
both Cleveland and McKinley had told me of their
dislike for him, but his record as a soldier and Indian

fighter was greatly in his favor. I repeated the G. A. R. veterans' admiration for the general.

He said: "Secretary Root dislikes him as much as I do."

Finally I suggested, as the general had about a year to serve before his age limit expired, that he be sent around the world on an inspection tour of the world's armies, and when he returned it would take him some weeks to write his report; then his time would be up and he would drop out automatically.

Roosevelt said: "That's a bully idea. I want you to tell it to Root. I will ask him to come to your hotel to-morrow morning early, so you can catch the 10.50 train for Chicago."

About 9 o'clock Sunday morning the Secretary of War rang me up and said the President had asked him to see me at the Arlington, but there would be some danger of newspaper men in the lobby, and asked me if I would not put my satchel in a cab and come to his home en route to the depot.

I did so, and told him I was greatly embarrassed to make suggestions to him, and asked if the President had told him of our talk the night before. He said: "Yes; in his careful, quiet way he told me the whole thing over the telephone! Although I do not feel as strongly as the President does over Miles, I think your suggestion a wise one."

Some days later the press announced General Miles

was sailing from San Francisco to inspect the armies of the world and make a report to the government on his return.

When the general reached the Philippines he gave a number of orders to the military officials in Manila, which they cabled to the War Department. The orders were promptly countermanded as soon as the general left the islands!

On his arrival in the United States, February 1, 1903, he wrote his report, and retired by age limit August 8, 1903.

The general probably knows now for the first time how it happened that he went around the world!

XXIV

PRESIDENT ROOSEVELT AND THE SPANISH FRIARS

WHEN Admiral Dewey took over the Philippines in 1898 he gave this government its first experience with the Catholic Church. The Spanish friars had complete control of the lands, souls, and bodies of the Filipinos.

The friars were a great source of irritation to President McKinley, President Roosevelt, and the United States officials in the islands. As stated in a previous chapter, President McKinley once remarked to me: "If old Dewey had only sailed out of the harbor of Manila after he had sunk the Spanish fleet, he would have saved us a lot of trouble!"

August 4, 1902, I received the following telegram from Oyster Bay:

The President would be pleased to have you lunch with him here Thursday, August 7, at half past one. Answer.   (Signed) WILLIAM LOEB, JR.,
                                    Acting Secretary.

I wired acceptance. After luncheon Roosevelt and I went out on the lawn and sat in the shade of a tree. He said: "Old man, I am in the worst hole politically I have ever been in my life. The whole Catholic Church is on my back, and you know how impossible it is to fight that great organization. You know what a lecherous lot of scoundrels the Spanish friars are in the Philippines. We are receiving constant reports from our officials stationed there complaining of the friars and the disturbances they cause among the natives. Of course these reports are confidential and are not published, but there are Catholics in the War Department, and through them the reports leak out. The day I wired you, John D. Crimmins, of New York, came to see me. He became very violent of speech, and said that the reports of the immorality of the friars were lies and were simply propaganda to establish Protestant missions in the Philippines. He defended the friar, and said he was under the dominion of the Pope at Rome, the same as the priests of Oyster Bay or Washington. That these calumnies must cease or the Catholics would see to it that I did not receive the nomination in 1904, and if I was nominated they would do everything in their power to defeat me. He practically shook his fist under my nose. I told him that he was mistaken; that the reports were sent in by the officials without any desire to reflect on the Catholic Church or to start propaganda for Protestant schools and churches, but he would not listen to any explanations, and left me in very great anger."

After some minutes of talk, I suggested he send a Catholic priest to the Philippines to make an investigation and report to the government. He said: "How can I send a Catholic priest? I am not the Pope." "No, you are not the Pope, but you have Catholic priests in the army, and," I continued, "there is one man that I know, Father E. J. Vattmann, who will go if he receives orders, and will make a truthful report. Let me tell you an incident that took place in Ohio in 1893." I then related the part Captain Vattmann played in defeating the A. P. A. fight against McKinley for the governorship in 1894, which I relate in the previous chapter, "McKinley and the A. P. A." in 1893.

I suggested he ask Secretary of War Root to invite Captain Father Vattmann, who was at that time stationed at Fort Sheridan, Ill., to come to Washington, and ask him to go to the Philippines with a company which was sailing in a few days. I told him that Captain Vattmann had lately returned from the Philippines because the climate did not agree with him, and that if he consented to go again, to request Governor Taft to give Father Vattmann a roving commission; when he was through his investigations to allow him to return to the United States.

A few days later Captain Vattmann came into my room in the Record-Herald Building in Chicago and showed me a letter he had received from Secretary

Root asking him to come to Washington as soon as possible. Captain Vattmann said: "That's a pretty important letter for a little fellow like me to get. I wonder what he wants?" I answered: "Well, you must report for duty. He probably has some mission he wants to intrust to you."

On his return from Washington and his visit to Secretary Root, Vattmann said: "They want me to go to the Philippines to investigate the trouble the government is having with the friars, and to verify, if possible, the charges of their immorality."

About three months later Vattmann came into my office on his return from the Philippines and showed me a little memorandum book giving details of towns he had visited and the dates. He told me he did not know there was so much wickedness in the world as was practised by the Spanish friars. He said they kept from two to four women apiece in their parish houses, and one friar with whom he stopped several days became very friendly and, knowing the captain was an army man and "hail-fellow-well-met," suggested that if he saw any woman in the congregation that pleased his fancy, he would send her to his room. He also told me the natives despised and hated the Spanish friars, and had killed some seventy of them in the last few years, principally because they violated their wives and daughters.

After resting a few days from his long journey, Father Vattmann proceeded to Washington to lay his report before Secretary Root. On his return he told me Mr. Root said: "Your report is the same as we have been getting for years, and we do not know how to remedy the situation." Captain Vattmann, a fearless, honest Christian, said: "I know how to settle the trouble." "What are you going to do?" "I am going to Baltimore to lay the whole matter before Cardinal Gibbons."

Father Vattmann told me that when he got on the train at Washington to go to Baltimore, he was told by the train conductor that Cardinal Gibbons was in the chair-car. He went back and found him asleep, and took a chair opposite him. When the cardinal awoke he said: "Why, Vattmann, I thought you were in the Philippines." "I was, Your Eminence, but have just returned, and am on my way to Baltimore to tell you of the awful conditions I found."

He spent the night with Cardinal Gibbons, and gave him a full report of all he had seen and heard. The pure-minded cardinal was horrified and said: "I want you to come back in two weeks and tell this awful state of affairs to the trustees of the Catholic University of Washington."

Two weeks later Father Vattmann appeared before the archbishops, and for two hours was cross-questioned. They were also horrified, and said:

"The Holy Father must know this. The Catholic Church of America teaches purity of thought and conduct. We have a large body of troops in the Philippines, and 60 per cent of them are Catholics. The terrible example of the friars will demoralize them. When they come home it will spread like a cancer throughout the youth of the church. It must not be."

Some weeks later Father Vattmann came into my room and showed me a telegram from Archbishop Ireland, which read:

Go to Mr. Kohlsaat; get what money you need and leave for Rome at once to see the Holy Father.

I was surprised that they asked me, the son of a Baptist minister, to pay the expenses of a priest to Rome! However, I loaned Father Vattmann $500, which he added to $400 of his own. He repaid the loan some three or four months later.

April 24, 1903, the New York *Sun* printed a despatch from Washington dated April 23, stating that the archbishop of the Catholic hierarchy had commissioned Father Vattmann to carry his report to Rome, etc. On May 31, 1903, the New York *Tribune* shows Captain Vattmann in Rome, presenting his report to the Pope on May 30, 1903.

Father Vattmann presented himself at the Vatican and had an audience with Pope Leo. I have been told it is a rule of the Catholic Church that one priest or order cannot complain against another to the Holy Father, and that was the reason why Father Vattmann came to me for the necessary funds to proceed to Rome. There, as a CAPTAIN OF THE UNITED STATES ARMY, with the shoulder-straps of a captain, he told the Holy Father of what he found in the Philippines.

Governor Taft of the Philippines, now Chief Justice Taft, was in Rome in June and July, 1903, negotiating with the Vatican under instructions from President Roosevelt and Secretary Root. President Roosevelt, in order to avoid a great scandal which would reflect on the Catholic Church, concluded the only way to avoid a scandal was for the United States to buy out the friars. He conferred with Senator Aldrich, chairman of the Senate Appropriation Committee, and Uncle Joe Cannon, of the House of Representatives. They promised him they would see that an appropriation of $7,000,000 was voted to buy the friar lands.

Governor Taft began negotiations with Pope Leo. They continued until His Holiness died, July 16, 1903, and were resumed by Pope Pius X on his accession to the papal throne, August 9, 1903.

The United States finally came into possession, and over 360 friars were thrown off the island. Father Vattmann said he never knew what became of them.

Our government sent Archbishop Harty, of St. Louis, to take charge of the churches and schools, of course with the Pope's consent. At the suggestion of the archbishop 1,000 American Catholic school-teachers were sent to the island.

Captain Vattmann, by age limit, was to retire from active service September 11, 1904. Some months before I asked him if there was anything the government could do for him. "I would like to be a major and receive a major's pay—$2,300 a year. I have purchased a little house for my niece and her husband in Willamette, Ill., paying part down. If I get $2,300 a year, in time I can pay for it." I said: "Is there such a rank in the army for chaplains?" "No; it would have to be by congressional action."

I took the matter up with President Roosevelt, Secretary of War Root, and Speaker Cannon. They promised the necessary legislation.

On April 20, 1904, Captain Vattmann came to me and said: "They have done nothing in Congress about my commission, and Congress adjourns to-morrow."

I wired Roosevelt, Root, and Cannon they had not kept their word with Vattmann, and that it must be done before adjournment, or it would be too late. In the closing hours of Congress, April 21, 1904, the rank of major for army chaplains was created. To avoid criticism a Protestant was also appointed along with Captain Vattmann, who retired with the rank of major September 11, 1904.

In later years President Roosevelt and President Taft gave Father Vattmann full charge of the Filipino students in this country.

He was unfortunate enough to break a leg and was sent to the Catholic Hospital in Evanston, Ill., where he was visited by ex-President Roosevelt and ex-President Taft.

On the entry of this country into the great World War, Major Vattmann, at seventy-five, offered his services to the government, and they were accepted. He again donned his beloved uniform, and did splendid work in the hospital at Fort Sheridan, Ill.   His cheery disposition did much to lighten the pain of many a soldier boy.

The church fully appreciated the great services of Major Vattmann, and created him a monsignor on the fiftieth anniversary of his priesthood.

Major Vattmann died September 29, 1919.   The funeral was held in the Holy Name Cathedral and was attended by all the military officials in Illinois, Governor Lowden, and thousands who mourned the loss of a friend who, in a single step, rose from a modest priest to a monsignor.

XXV

PRESIDENT ROOSEVELT AND JAMES STILLMAN

On my return from Oyster Bay, August 7, 1902, I received a telegram from Mr. James Stillman, president of the National City Bank, New York, asking me to dine with him that evening. I broke an engagement and telephoned acceptance. Mr. Stillman lived in East 72d Street.

Mr. Stillman, his son James A., and myself were the only people at the table. The house was in summer garb, the furniture covered with linen. The menu card was placed at Mr. Stillman's plate, and after each course he made a notation—"Good," "Indifferent," or "Bad," which he told the butler to hand to the chef. The procedure amused me, as I thought it was all "Good."

After dinner Mr. Stillman took me into another room and said: "I suppose you are wondering why I invited you here to dinner on a hot August night?" I said: "Yes; I have been puzzled ever since I came into the house."

"Well, I am going to be very frank with you. Frank Vanderlip says that you are very close to

President Roosevelt; that you visited him to-day at Oyster Bay. The truth is that the country is in a very bad financial condition. There are several banks in New York City on the verge of failure. They are full of what J. P. Morgan calls 'undigested securities.' We have had several meetings of financial men to discuss the situation. We cabled Mr. Morgan to come home from Europe. It was finally decided that if President Roosevelt would order the Secretary of the Treasury, Shaw, to put out $20,000,-000 or $25,000,000 of government deposits, based on New England Savings Banks' securities instead of government bonds, and place the money in the banks of the West, Northwest, and Southwest, to move the crops, and let New York stew in its own juice, we can pull through. If the President will do this, and keep the country banks from drawing on New York banks for accommodations, it will relieve the situation greatly. We in turn will pull the stops from under stocks and put them all on a 5 per cent basis. When the latter proposition was discussed, Mr. Morgan roared like a bull, because it would hit his pet baby, United States Steel Common, which pays no dividend, but is selling around 40. The stock will probably drop to 8 or 10. But Mr. Morgan took a sensible view of it and agreed to the plan." I said: "Well, what has this got to do with me? Why do not you or some of the other big Wall

Street men go to Oyster Bay and lay the matter before Roosevelt?" He said: "If Mr. Morgan or I went to Roosevelt it would bring on a panic, because the country would know that nothing short of a serious situation would prompt us to do such a thing. Can you imagine how Theodore Roosevelt would crack his teeth with joy to have us call on him for help?"

I told him I was going to Boston to see my father-in-law, E. Nelson Blake, but would write Roosevelt that night and tell him of the interview. If he wanted to see me to wire me at Boston and I would return to New York.

Sunday I received a telegram from the President asking me to return to Oyster Bay on Monday.

When I told Roosevelt of my interview with Stillman, his face was a study. He did not attempt to conceal his dislike for the big men in Wall Street, and said: "By George, how I would like to get a chance to smash those fellows!" I replied: "The trouble is you would smash the whole country in the operation, and a lot of innocent people would suffer."

Roosevelt said he would telegraph Secretary Shaw to come to Oyster Bay at once. A few days later, after seeing the President, the Secretary issued a statement that he would put out $20,000,000 to $25,000,000 of government deposits, based on New England Savings Banks' securities, and if that was not enough to move the crops, he would put out $25,000,000 more.

When Secretary Shaw's statement was published, the president of one of the big Chicago banks said to me that it was like the "breaking of a boil"!

The national banking law makes government bonds the only basis for government deposits, but President Roosevelt and Secretary Shaw showed great courage in acting to prevent a panic. There was no risk involved, as the New England Savings Banks' law gives close scrutiny to the bonds and stocks the New England banks are allowed to purchase or loan on.

Secretary Shaw's action led to the passage of the Vreeland-Aldrich Bill, which made the use of New England Savings Banks' securities legal.

Mr. Stillman was right about the effect of pulling the stops from under United States Steel Common. It went to 8⅜ within a few months.

XXVI

GOVERNOR LESLIE M. SHAW

It may interest Governor Leslie M. Shaw, of Iowa, to learn how he came to be appointed Secretary of the Treasury in Roosevelt's cabinet.

Here's the story:

Secretary Lyman J. Gage promised President Roosevelt on the arrival of the train bearing President McKinley's body to Washington that he would stay a few months until his successor was chosen.

In December, 1901, I discussed 1904 nominations with Roosevelt. At that time the only opposition in sight was Governor Shaw, of Iowa, whose stanch advocacy of the gold standard at St. Louis in 1896 made him a conspicuous figure. He stood almost alone against bimetallism; the balance of the Iowa delegation were very wabbly.

There was considerable sentiment for him for President in 1904 in Iowa, the two Dakotas, and Nebraska. He was also popular with the financial element in the East, who feared Roosevelt.

I suggested to the President he offer the treasury portfolio to Governor Shaw. The idea sank in.

About a week later I received a telegram from Governor Shaw from Des Moines asking if I would

be in Chicago the next day. He wanted to see me.
When he came he showed me President Roosevelt's
telegram, offering him the secretaryship of the
treasury. I was very much surprised, but strongly
advised him to accept. He went to Dubuque, consulted Senator Allison, wired his acceptance, and
was appointed January 6, 1902.

XXVII

PRESIDENT ROOSEVELT AND "BOZZIE"

In March, 1902, I took supper in the White House with the President, Mrs. Roosevelt, and her three little boys—Kermit, Archie, and Quentin. I think little Ethel was at school. I told them of a collie dog named "Bozzie," owned by a Mr. Clason, an ex-conductor on the Chicago and Northwestern Railroad.

Bozzie was a mind-reader. That statement may be questioned by people not familiar with this wonderful dog, but no other explanation accounts for the marvellous acts she performed. The children were interested but incredulous. Finally Quentin said: "Father, did you ever hear of a dog that could do such things?" Roosevelt said: "No, Quentin, I never did, but you must remember Mr. Kohlsaat is a newspaper man!" I replied: "In other words, I am a 'fibber'! I will send Mr. Clason and Bozzie down here and let you judge for yourself."

Some weeks later Mr. Clason agreed to go to Washington and take Bozzie, if I would pay his expenses! I agreed, and it cost me over $300 to make good!

On May 9, 1902, Mrs. Roosevelt wrote me the following letter:

The children are looking forward to the visit of the wonderful "Bozzie" and I write to ask if it can be made on Friday, the 16th. My little Ethel goes to school at Woodley and only comes home on Friday and spends Sunday with me. Of course I can make a special arrangement for her to be here on Thursday, but if it is not absolutely necessary, I do not like to ask them to put aside the rules for her. I was so glad to see your daughter with Mrs. Noyes yesterday. Please be sure not to change "Bozzie's" date, if it is at all inconvenient.

Sincerely yours,

EDITH K. ROOSEVELT.

When Mr. Clason returned to Chicago, he said the President was deeply interested in Bozzie's performance. After watching her for some time, he got down on the floor and took her in his arms and hugged her, as he would a child. He ordered the Secret Service to detail a man to watch and follow Bozzie while she was in Washington.

Soon after I received the following letter from Roosevelt:

WHITE HOUSE
WASHINGTON

May 24, 1902

MY DEAR MR. KOHLSAAT:

That dog is far more wonderful than any animal I have ever seen (Senator Hanna is listening and wishes me to add that she knows more than you do, which remark I refuse to endorse.) I am really awfully obliged to you for having given us a chance to see the remarkable performance. Good luck to you.

Faithfully yours,

THEODORE ROOSEVELT.

P. S. Senator Hanna is now leaning out of the window looking at the dog going through her performance on the portico at the rear of the White House. It is positively uncanny!

Bozzie was about to become a mother when I told the children of her wonders in March. I asked the boys if they would like one of her puppies, if Mr. Clason would give me one, and received the following letter from Kermit:

WHITE HOUSE

WASHINGTON

April 14, 1902

DEAR MR. KOHLSAAT:

I should just love if Mr. Clason would give me one of the little puppies. I would prefer a male. Will you tell Mr. Clason that the 15th will suit us splendidly. I think the last authunatic example is the wonderful.

How are your daughters' dogs? We all look forward to seeing "Bozzie" awfully.

Yours sincerely,

KERMIT ROOSEVELT.

Mr. Clason sent one of the puppies to Kermit at Oyster Bay in the early summer. They called him Bozzie after his wonderful mother.

One afternoon, when the children were at school,

President Roosevelt said to me: "Come into the nursery. I want to show you some of the children's pets." We went across the hall from the old cabinet room into the nursery, where there were two or three little beds. Roosevelt went into a corner, and brought out a big piebald rat, with a tail some six or eight inches long. He put the animal on his shoulder. It walked around his collar, its rough, file-like tail scraping his neck. I can feel to this day the chill it sent down my backbone. He offered to let me hold "Jonathan," but I declined! He replaced the rat in the box and took a macaw off his perch and held him on his finger. "Eli" had a beak that would bite through a piece of steel. Roosevelt said: "Archie lets Eli stand on his shoulder, and he reaches down and nips off the buttons of his coat, as if they were a piece of cheese, and wants to have him sit on my shoulders, but I am afraid he would bite off an ear with as much ease. Archie calls me a 'coward.' Says: 'You call yourself the hero of San Juan Hill, and yet you are afraid of a bird! You're a coward!'"

One day while in the Blue Room I heard a clatter of hoofs on the floor of the entrance to the White House. I left the room in time to see Archie and I. H. Hoover trying to persuade a small pony to get into the elevator and go up to the nursery. After considerable hauling and pushing they succeeded.

Mr. Hoover has charge of the White House and,

April 14. 1902

Dear Mr Ashlear.

I should just love

if Mr Clason would give me one of

the little puppies I would prefer a male.

Will you tell Mr Clason that the 15th

will suit us splendidly.

I think the last automatic example

is the wonderful.

How are your daughter's dogs.

We all look forward to seeing Bossie

awfully.   Yours sincerely

Kermit Roosevelt

as a cabinet officer once said to me, "tells the President what to do. He is the real ruler of the White House." Mr. Hoover was appointed by President Harrison in 1891, and is still on duty, efficient and courteous as ever.

One night the President and I were in the library. Archie came into the room on a pair of very high stilts. He stalked around on the slippery rugs, with the usual result. As he fell, one of the stilts smashed a large lamp-shade on the library table. The boy hurt himself and whimpered, but pluckily restrained from crying. I was curious to see what punishment was coming. Screwing up his mouth, Roosevelt said, "Archie, I think you had better confine your peregrinations to the hall," and resumed conversation as though nothing had happened.

The life of the Roosevelt family in the White House was beautiful. I believe there have never been so many children romping through its halls since it was built. The President and his children were pals.

There may be gentler, sweeter mothers in the world than Mrs. Roosevelt, but I never knew one.

XXVIII

ROOSEVELT HUNTING 1904 DELEGATES

DURING the winter of 1902 and 1903 President Roosevelt negotiated the Reciprocity Treaty with Cuba. The Louisiana sugar interests fought the treaty, as they believed it menaced the sugar-growers of the South. After much discussion the treaty passed, March 9, 1903.

In February, 1903, I spent an evening in the White House. Mrs. Roosevelt and the children were at the supper-table. The only outside guests were Nicholas Murray Butler and myself. The children carried on an animated conversation among themselves. Roosevelt, Doctor Butler, and I were deeply engrossed at the other end of the table discussing the Cuban Treaty, when Archie broke in with, "Father, *Father*, FATHER," louder each time. "What is it, Archie?" exclaimed the President. "Father, doesn't the monkey-cage at the Zoo smell terrible?" "My recollection is that it does, Archie!"

Before going in to supper I asked the President how he was getting along, and he replied: "With the Cuban Reciprocity Treaty on my hands and at the same time being father of Alice Roosevelt, I am doing pretty well!"

Roosevelt was very anxious for the nomination for President in 1904. His three and a half years serving out McKinley's term had given him a taste of being Chief Executive. He had carried out McKinley's policies, and naturally wanted an opportunity to try some of his own. There was little opposition to him. Mark Hanna was the only name mentioned. Some anti-Roosevelt people tried to get Hanna to become a candidate. He gave them no encouragement. First, because he was in poor health and, second, he believed Roosevelt was entitled to what was practically a second term.

Roosevelt in his great desire to be nominated sent for politicians whom he thought had influence in their respective States, in several cases ignoring the senators and representatives. The Ohio delegation in Congress were mad because he invited the vice-mayor, as they called him, of Cincinnati to come to Washington and lunch with him. A number of other politicians were asked to the White House for lunch or dinner. His fear was unwarranted, for when the national committee met in Washington, December 11, 1903, to choose the convention city, and set the date, they were practically unanimous for Roosevelt, as Mark Hanna by letter and personal contact had declined to be considered a candidate and strongly advised the nomination of Roosevelt.

A few days after the national committee was in

session I arrived in Washington; the first man I met in the Arlington Hotel lobby was Senator Aldrich, of Rhode Island. He said: "I wish you could persuade your friend in the White House to quit his hunt for delegates; he is making a damned fool of himself." Two well-known correspondents made similar remarks.

I went to the White House about 5 o'clock. The President was out riding. Saw Secretary Loeb and told him what the three men had said to me. He said: "I have talked with him, but it is no use. I cannot do anything with him. Wish you would talk to him." Mr. Loeb said he would try to arrange for an interview on the President's return from a cabinet dinner. Later I received a note asking me to come to the White House at 10.30 that night.

The President came in with a rush. Saw Mrs. Roosevelt to the elevator and joined me. We went up the marble-and-iron stairway opposite the Blue Room. As we went up the stairs Roosevelt said: "I have been in hell for the last three or four weeks!" I replied: "Yes, and you have acted like it!" He said: "What do you mean?" "Wait until we get on the landing. You might throw me over the banisters!"

After looking over some papers on his desk he said: "What did you mean by that remark?" I replied: "The first man I met in the hotel on my

arrival said you were making a damned fool of yourself in your quest for delegates. The second one
said you were acting like a jackass. The third said
you were crazy, and from what I learn all three were
right. You are sending for men to come to Washington and inviting them to lunch or dinner—men
unworthy to sit at the White House table. I met
one from the South this afternoon in Loeb's office.
He is a scalawag. I know him. He told me he
lunched with you to-day. These men give out interviews to their home papers before coming to Washington, boasting of your invitation. They give
statements to the Washington correspondents telling
of dining with you. Then you talk to them and ask
for their support. After leaving you they walk
straight across Lafayette Square and tell Mark
Hanna everything you said. You say Hanna is
'scrootching' a little. He is not. Mr. Hanna is
a very sick man. I doubt very much whether he
will be alive in June when the convention meets,
but if you keep this thing up you will disgust everybody and lose the nomination."

The President jumped to his feet. I got up also.
He said: "Sit down, sit down. I don't like to have
my feelings hurt any more than anybody else, but
it takes the brutal frankness of a friend to crystallize
a resolution. I will refuse to discuss delegates with
any one, and will begin on a delegation waiting

down-stairs right now! In the morning I will give a statement to the press to that effect."

Next morning before leaving for Chicago I went to the White House and asked Major Loeffler, the veteran who guards the President's door, to ask the President if I could see him a moment. Roosevelt met me half-way across the room. I said: "Last night after I went to bed it came over me that I had talked very harsh not only to a dear friend but to the President of the United States, and I want to apologize." Roosevelt pointed to Secretary Root, who was sitting on a sofa going over some papers with Secretary Loeb, and said: "Do you see that man over there? He and you are the two most brutal friends I have and the two I pay the most attention to. The first thing I did this morning was to hand a statement to the press."

Mark Hanna failed rapidly. I saw him a few days before he died, February 15, 1904. He told me the President came to see him and brought flowers from the White House. With his eyes filled with tears he said: "He sits by the bed and holds my hand just as if I was a girl. I hear from him every day."

And Mark Hanna had a little hand, just like a woman's.

XXIX

ROOSEVELT AND FAIRBANKS—1904

WHEN Mark Hanna died, February 15, 1904, no other name but Roosevelt was seriously mentioned for the Presidential nomination. Roosevelt and Fairbanks were nominated in Chicago, June 23, 1904.

The Democrats nominated Judge Alton B. Parker, of New York, for President, and Henry G. Davis, of West Virginia, for Vice-President.

Until the middle of September Judge Parker was thought to be sure of New York by 100,000 plurality. He was able, popular, and had the support of the New York *Times, World,* and the Democratic press of the country.

But in October reports came in to Republican headquarters that prominent Democrats in different sections of the country were showing a disposition to vote for Roosevelt. Men who had been hostile to him were changing their attitude and praising some of his administrative acts.

On his return to New York at the end of October, John J. Mitchell, president Illinois Trust & Savings Bank, Chicago, telephoned me an invitation to lunch with him. He said: "You remember telling me of your suggestion to Roosevelt to send Father Vattmann to investigate the immoralities of the Philippine friars in 1902? Well, I heard the echo of that in New York two or three days ago. I lunched with J. Edward Simmons, president of the Fourth National Bank, who is very close to some of the national Democratic committee. He told me of a meeting called in New York City about the middle of October by the State Democratic committee to apportion money necessary to man the polls. One after another of the county chairmen reported a great change of sentiment from Parker to Roosevelt. They said leading Catholic Democrats in their district had announced they would vote for Roosevelt, and were doing everything in their power to elect him, because of his action in the friar troubles in the Philippines after Captain Father Vattmann's investigation. They predicted Parker would lose the State by a large plurality instead of winning by 100,000 as was expected early in the campaign."

Such proved to be the case, as Roosevelt carried New York State by over 175,000 plurality. Parker only received some 40,000 plurality in New York City.

The same issue was one cause of Roosevelt's tremendous plurality in the country.

The Catholics are 85 per cent Democrats, and

when they change to the Republican ticket their influence is greatly felt.

Roosevelt had over 2,500,000 plurality. It was the religious issue which largely contributed to his great victory.

It has been said by wise political leaders that if Roosevelt had gone to Genoa instead of Rome on his return from Africa he would have come much nearer winning from Wilson in 1912.

When the election returns were received November 8, 1904, showing Roosevelt's overwhelming majority, he issued a statement through the Associated Press as follows:

I am deeply sensible of the honor done me by the American people in thus expressing their confidence in what I have done and have tried to do.

I appreciate to the full the solemn responsibility this confidence imposes on me, and I shall do all that lies in my power not to forfeit it.

On the 4th of March next I shall have served three and one half years and the three and one half years constitute my first term.

The wise custom which limits the President to two terms regards the substance and not the form, and under no circumstances will I be a candidate for or accept another nomination.

This totally unnecessary voluntary statement prevented Roosevelt from accepting renomination for a second term. He was filling out the unexpired term of President McKinley, but his definite statement that under no circumstances would he be a candidate for or accept another nomination made it impossible, with his code of honor, to break his word, as much as he deplored having made the promise.

He said to me once, "I would cut my hand off right there," putting his finger on his wrist, "if I could recall that written statement!"

XXX

ROOSEVELT AND THE CHICAGO TEAM-
STERS' STRIKE, 1905

In April, 1905, President Roosevelt made a trip
through the South and West, ending in a bear and
lion hunt in the Rockies of Colorado. The party
shot ten bear. There is no record of any mountain
lions.

Sunday, May 7, he returned to Glenwood Springs,
leaving for Chicago the next morning to get the day-
light ride through Colorado. He arrived in Chicago
Wednesday morning, May 10.

For some weeks Chicago had been in the throes of
anarchy caused by the teamsters' strike, led by Cornelius P. Shea, president of the International Brother-
hood of Teamsters.

An employers' association was formed to break the
strike. Business was completely paralyzed as far as
horse service was concerned. All sorts of outrages
were perpetrated on the few animals appearing on
the street. Light shells filled with sulphuric acid
were thrown from windows on the horses. Stables
were entered and horses' tongues cut off.

Mayor Dunne was powerless to stop the disorder.

When it was published that Roosevelt was coming
the employers' association appointed a committee

to meet him early Wednesday morning at Sterling, Ill. The teamsters' committee went them one better and appointed some of their number to meet Roosevelt at Clinton, Iowa, about daybreak.

I wrote Roosevelt a letter to reach him Sunday morning at Glenwood Springs, Colo., as he came out of the mountains. I told him of the plans to meet him and warned him not to commit himself until he knew all the details. On receipt of my letter Sunday morning he wired Chicago he would receive no committee on the train, and sent me a telegram to meet him at De Kalb, Ill., on arrival of his train at 7 o'clock, A. M. I did so.

Several hundred people were applauding his speech as he stood on the rear platform of his train. Frank Tyree, Roosevelt's bodyguard, took me in the front door of his private car. When the train started we sat down for breakfast, and I told Roosevelt of the strike. He knew nothing of it, except a small item he had seen in a Colorado paper.

I told him the teamsters' officials met in a disreputable house known as "The Old Kentucky Home" on Indiana Avenue, drank champagne with the inmates, and were constantly under the influence of liquor to give them "Dutch courage." They knew they were whipped and wanted an excuse to let go. They were going to ask him to suggest arbitration to save their faces. I told him there could be no arbitration with the drunken scoundrels. They deserved no consideration whatever.

The teamsters had asked for a meeting that afternoon in the Congress Hotel, where Roosevelt was stopping. I advised him to see them, but to have Billy Loeb and a stenographer present to take down all that was said by both parties to prevent any misquoting by the teamsters after he had left town, and then give them h——l! He did so in true Rooseveltian style!

I also told him the Merchants' Club was to give him a luncheon, and asked him to say nothing of the strike, as it was beneath the dignity of his office to take a hand in a teamsters' strike; that he was to be the dinner guest of the Iroquois Club, a Democratic organization, and sit next to Mayor Dunne; and, to put some backbone into that official, asked him when called on for a speech to say as a preface:

Mayor Dunne, in your efforts to suppress disorder and strife you have my heartiest sympathy and support. If you need assistance call on the Governor of the State. If he needs assistance call on the United States Government.

Roosevelt looked at the envelope on which I had written the above, and said:

I know what I will say: Mayor Dunne, in your efforts to suppress disorder and strife you have my heartiest sympathy and support. Remember—back of the City stands the State. Back of the State the Nation.

What he did say at the banquet follows:

Mr. Mayor, as President of the United States and therefore as representative of the people of this country, I give you as a matter of course my hearty support in upholding the law, in keeping order, in putting down violence, whether by mob or by an individual. There need not be the slightest apprehension in the heart of the most timid that ever mob spirit will triumph in this country. Those immediately responsible for dealing with the trouble must, as I know you feel, exhaust every effort in so dealing with it before a call is made upon an outside body, but if ever the need arises *back of the City stands the State and back of the State stands the Nation.*

The effect on the diners was electrical. They jumped on their chairs, cheered, and waved their napkins. Some in their enthusiasm wanted to hoist Roosevelt on their shoulders! When quiet was restored, he made the set speech he had prepared and handed to the press.

Next day the strike collapsed, and Roosevelt received the just praise he deserved from all over the country.

The New York *Times*, which was never overpartial to Roosevelt, printed the following editorial:

RESPECT FOR THE LAW

The reply of President Roosevelt to the representative of the striking teamsters of Chicago, was dignified, intelligent and to the point. What is especially to be com-

From a photograph, copyright Pirie MacDonald

PRESIDENT ROOSEVELT

mended in it was the avoidance of any generalization which could be construed into an expression of sympathy with the attitude of the men, who, to accomplish a purpose, are maintaining the condition of anarchy in a great city.

It would have been very easy for the President to say something intended to be emollient, which would have admitted of distortion into an expression of sympathy with their aims and means, etc., etc.

Before Roosevelt reached Washington he sent me a telegram:

> On train, May 11th, 1905.
> Our speech went great, didn't it?
> THEODORE ROOSEVELT.

XXXI

ROOSEVELT HATED OBSCENITY

GENERAL U. S. GRANT and Theodore Roosevelt had one characteristic in common—they both hated obscenity or off-colored stories.

It is told of General Grant that after the ladies had left the dinner-table and the coffee and cigars were brought in, one of the guests said: "As there are no ladies present, I want to tell a story." Before he could begin it, Grant quietly said, "But there are gentlemen present," completely squelching the man and his story.

One of the newspaper men who accompanied President Roosevelt on his trip to the Colorado bear hunt came to Chicago with him May 10, 1905. He told me of an experience they had in San Antonio, Texas, where the President stopped off to attend a Rough Riders' reunion.

The people of San Antonio tendered him a banquet. One of the prominent merchants of the city was toastmaster. He attempted a coarse parody on the President's crusade on race suicide. He made a play upon the nursery rhyme relating to "the old woman who lived in a shoe, who had so many children she didn't know what to do," and compared

144

her lot with modern woman in a manner that was hardly a parlor story.

Ordinarily the President sat through the most fulsome praise without in the least betraying his thoughts. This dinner was given on the ground floor of the old Menger Hotel. In the windows and filling the patio were the wives and other guests of the diners. The President looked up with a sharp jerk of his head; his teeth clicked, his jaw was set, and for a moment it looked as if he intended to interrupt the speaker. But it was only for a moment. He then turned to the neighbor on his right and from that time on listened no more to the speaker, but continued an animated conversation. When the speaker sat down on the President's left he was not congratulated, but was ignored. When the President spoke later in the evening he did not refer to the toastmaster in any way except that he referred to the speaker who had made an unfortunate choice of a place to give expression to a poem which he hoped was home-made.

XXXII

DANGER IN ROOSEVELT'S HUNTING TRIP

MY newspaper friend said there was a big responsibility taken by those accompanying Roosevelt on his hunting trip.

Many people considered that the President had no right to risk his life in such dangerous undertakings as hunting bears and mountain lions. The President recognized this argument made by his supporters and close personal advisers, and constantly replied to these arguments that he was not taking half the supposed risk nor was he nearly so daring as he was credited with being.

The President's train stopped at Newcastle, Colo. It was from that point the hunting party planned to enter the mountain region where bears were supposed to range. The newspaper men on the trip were busy getting off a story when a messenger summoned them to the President's car. The President said: "You boys may be tempted to exaggerate the risks I am running out here. A few years ago I was hunting mountain lions, and one of the newspaper men wrote a bully story, picturing me hanging over a cliff by my toes and fighting a mountain lion with nothing but a naked knife. Judging from some of

the protests I received, people did not like it.   There
was no Vice-President then, and probably my life
was worth more than it is now."

The President chuckled and told, not for quota-
tion, Finley Peter Dunne's ("Mr. Dooley's") quip,
that "if Roosevelt had to go down in a submarine,
he hoped he would please take Vice-President Fairbanks along with him!"

The President said he had promised his friends
he would take no chances of a bear getting hold of
him on the trip.   Resuming his admonition to the
correspondents and operating his pump-gun in such
a manner as to show it was in perfect order, he said:
"Now you fellows can keep this in mind.   If you
get hard up for a story don't write anything about
my running risks.   Just remember that I intend to
keep this weapon between me and danger."

"Nevertheless, Colonel Roosevelt," continued my
newspaper friend, "had to be pretty sharply watched
by his hosts in order to keep him out of danger.   Before we reached Colorado he went on a jack-rabbit
and wolf hunt over territory that is now Oklahoma.
His host was the late Cecil Lyon, then Republican
national committeeman for Texas, and one of Roosevelt's friends in his cowboy days.   Another member
of the party was Jack Abernethy, the man who
'caught 'em alive.'   Jack used to chase wolves and
run them until he tired them out.   Then he would

hop off his horse, and as they would snap at him he quickly grabbed them around the lower jaw with his hand well back of their fangs. No other man did it, and Roosevelt had great admiration for him. He rode with Abernethy for hours one day just to see him perform that trick.

"Another stunt performed by Abernethy seemed even more startling, but Abernethy pooh-poohed the suggestion that there was any danger in it. He would stir up rattlesnakes until they became angry enough to strike. As they would coil and raise their heads rigidly to a height of several inches—which he said they always did before striking—he would hit them sharply back of the head with his riding-whip. He never failed to kill them in this way.

"Lyon and Roosevelt were riding in a jack-rabbit chase one day when Lyon noticed the President sliding off his horse. He rode forward quickly to see if he could be of any assistance, and saw the President getting ready with his quirt to tap a rattle-snake back of the ears. Lyon shot the snake and proceeded to lecture the President about the promise he had made not to run unnecessary risks. Incidentally, Roosevelt never could see much sport in a jack-rabbit chase. He could not see any fun in shooting at an animal's heels, and much preferred firing when he could see the whites of their 'eyes'!"

There was never another character like Roosevelt. Every newspaper man naturally cultivates his news sources, and here was a man who not only was the source of news but everything he did was news. My friend, who has told me so much about the Roosevelt trip, said he first heard the term "praise agent" as a synonym for "press agent" within a few weeks after he was assigned to the White House.

Senator Nathan B. Scott, of West Virginia, a Republican senator—who was miffed over patronage—came out of the White House one day in a boiling rage, and when accosted by a group of correspondents, all he would say was that it was useless for him to try to get a fair hearing from a bunch of "praise agents" such as you are!

The appellation "cuckoos" came into use soon after Roosevelt's second term began because he was surrounded by a large number of correspondents who were inclined to take without question any new tidbits Roosevelt scattered and play them unquestionably to the advantage of the President. Frequently the President would pass out suggestions of some course he might take on public questions, or legislation, and then he would watch for the public reaction. If it was favorable, he would proceed in accordance with the suggestion, and if unfavorable, he would not hesitate to reject it, absolutely.

In such instances some new correspondent would be left "holding the bag." The cub not long in Washington, awe-stricken by a White House assignment, would be likely to accept without reservation anything falling from the lips of the strenuous President. If in his thoughts Roosevelt had always been "Teddy," his fall was all the harder. His story very likely went to his home paper with all the positiveness he could put into his writing. If his paper accepted the story without qualification, and later public reaction was against the announced policy, the young correspondent was in for a call-down.

It was only the cub reporters that were ever misled, and Colonel Roosevelt expected the older correspondents to take care of the youngsters on such occasions, as they were usually ready to do.

A newly arrived correspondent for one of the leading Paris papers once interviewed Roosevelt, and sent a highly colored indiscreet cable to his paper. When it appeared in print the Associated Press agent in Paris cabled it back to this country. It created a tremendous furor. The Washington bureau of the Associated Press received a positive denial from Roosevelt that he ever gave the interview. It put the poor Frenchman in a very bad hole.

Two or three days after the denial I lunched with the President in the White House. He asked me if

I had seen his statement denying the interview. I said: "Yes, and I believe you said what the Frenchman sent to his paper, because you have said the same thing to me." Snapping his teeth, he replied: "Of course I said it, but I said it as Theodore Roosevelt and not as the President of the United States!"

XXXIII

MRS. McKINLEY'S FUNERAL

MRS. McKINLEY, widow of President McKinley, died May 26, 1907. I was in Washington on the 27th. President Roosevelt invited me to go with him to the funeral.

We left Washington the night of the 28th, arriving in Canton, Ohio, next day at noon. Vice-President Fairbanks, Secretary of State Elihu Root, James Wilson, Secretary of Agriculture, and William Loeb, Jr., secretary to the President, were in the President's car.

At breakfast next morning I sat on Roosevelt's right, Secretary Root at the other end of the table, Vice-President Fairbanks, Secretary Wilson, and Mr. Loeb in between. Roosevelt discussed the candidates to be nominated the next year. In a very loud whisper he said: "If I were given the absolute power to appoint, I would make Elihu Root President and Will Taft Chief Justice." He added: "Don't tell Root I said it!" Mr. Root made a funny little gesture but no comment.

President Roosevelt went to the Canton home of

Justice William R. Day, of the Supreme Court, and lunched with Vice-President Fairbanks, Secretary Root, Secretary of the Treasury Cortelyou, who was with Mrs. McKinley when she passed away, Secretary Wilson, Myron T. Herrick, Governor Harris, of Ohio, and Mr. Loeb.

After luncheon they went to the modest McKinley home, a short distance from Justice Day's. With the exception of the President's party and a few warm friends, only members of the family were present.

The casket was placed in what was known as the "campaign office," or parlor of the little home. The services, which were very simple, were conducted by Reverend Doctor Buxton of the Methodist Episcopal church. The same hymns that were sung at McKinley's funeral were rendered by the church choir. They were McKinley's favorites: "Nearer, my God, to Thee," "Lead, Kindly Light," "Beautiful Isle of Somewhere."

The house was filled with roses, Mrs. McKinley's favorite flower. The floral tributes were so great that many were taken direct to the receiving-vault in which they placed the casket to await transfer to the McKinley memorial tomb, which was not quite completed.

The Secret Service men received information that a brother of Czolgosz—the man who shot President

McKinley in Buffalo in 1901—was in Canton, and would attempt to kill Roosevelt. No chances were taken. The Presidential party left the house by a side door to avoid the crowd in front of the house. The rumor proved to be untrue, as Czolgosz had gone to New Castle, Penna., to place a wreath on his wife's grave.

Business in Canton was suspended and the public schools closed during the services.

Mrs. McKinley was born in 1847. Part of her education was obtained in a New York State college. Her father—Mr. Saxton—was the principal owner of the Stark County Bank. He believed a girl should be able to earn her own living. So his daughter, Ida (Mrs. McKinley), went into his bank as a clerk, and for a time was cashier. While there Major McKinley fell in love with her. He was a very handsome young lawyer of twenty-seven. He was superintendent of the Methodist Sunday-school. Miss Saxton was a teacher in a Presbyterian Sunday-school. It is said that one Sunday in parting to go to their respective Sunday-school classes, McKinley said: "I don't like these partings. I think we should go together after this." She replied: "So do I." After a short engagement they were married in 1870.

Christmas day, 1871, her daughter Katie was born; thirteen months later another daughter came, and was named Ida, after her mother. She only lived a few weeks, and six months later little Katie passed away.

The death of the children completely shattered Mrs. McKinley's health. She was never again a well woman.

After the birth of baby Ida, Mrs. McKinley suffered from epilepsy. She was subject to fainting spells, which lasted only a few minutes but were very distressing to witness. I was alone with her once when she fainted, and could not leave her to look for her maid, so I went behind her chair and pressed her temples, as I had seen McKinley do many times. When she became conscious I left the room, and sent a maid to her. Later she apologized to me for making what she called "a scene."

Mrs. McKinley was passionately fond of little children. She would beg mothers to let her hold their babies. In 1891 Major and Mrs. McKinley visited our home on Prairie Avenue, Chicago. Our youngest child, Katherine, now Mrs. Roger Shepard, of St. Paul, was not quite two years old. McKinley held her on his lap while Mrs. McKinley played with our eight-year-old daughter, Pauline, the present Mrs. Potter Palmer, of Chicago.

Baby Katherine went to sleep in McKinley's arms. When Mrs. McKinley noticed it she said: "Please let me have her. I love to hold a sleeping baby." McKinley gently placed the child in her arms, with the admonition: "Don't drop her."   Before the child woke up, tears were rolling down Mrs. McKinley's cheeks.

There never was a more devoted lover and husband than McKinley.   His first thought was always of his wife's comfort.   He paid her the most loving attention.

With the persistence which was a part of her disease, she insisted on going everywhere with him. He apparently never crossed her wishes.

At state dinners and receptions in the White House she was always present, unless too ill to leave her room.   She sat next to the President, on his left, if there was a distinguished guest present to whom the dinner was given.   Frequently the excitement was too much for her and she fainted.   She did not fall out of her chair, but became rigid.   The President would throw a handkerchief or napkin over her face and proceed with the conversation as though nothing had happened.   The guests would look away and pay no attention to the invalid.   When the spasm passed she would be taken to her room by her maid and the White House physician, Doctor Leonard Wood, now General Leonard Wood, governor of the Philippines.

Two or three years after McKinley's death I called on Mrs. McKinley in Canton.   Although it was a warm spring day, she sat in a chair over a register from which the heat poured, a frail figure in a plain black gown, her hair cut short and curled at the ends.

Over and over she moaned: "Why should I linger? Please, God, if it is Thy will, let me go. I want to be with him. I am so tired."

XXXIV

ROOSEVELT AT McKINLEY'S TOMB

SEPTEMBER 29, 1907, Roosevelt, accompanied by his secretary, William Loeb, Jr., left Washington to inspect the Great-Lakes-to-Gulf deep-waterway project and to spend a couple of weeks in the canebrakes of Louisiana hunting bear. His first stop next morning was at Canton, Ohio, to dedicate the McKinley monument and mausoleum.

He was greeted by a crowd of 50,000 people. As he rode toward the monument he said it reminded him of a Greek temple.

Justice William R. Day, president of the McKinley National Memorial Association, presided, and told of the building of the monument by the contributions of nearly a million people from all walks of life at a cost of $600,000.

He said the tomb held the bodies of President McKinley, Mrs. McKinley, and their two little girls.

At the close of Justice Day's address Miss Helen McKinley, the only sister of the late President, drew aside the flag disclosing the bronze figure of McKinley in the attitude of delivering his last speech in Buffalo the day of his assassination, September 6, 1901.

The flag was removed slowly and impressively.

This was followed by the reading of the poem entitled "William McKinley," by James Whitcomb Riley.

The President, introduced by Governor Harris, was received with great applause. He said, in part:

We are gathered together to-day to pay our meed of respect to William McKinley, who as President won a place in the hearts of the American people such as but three or four of the Presidents of this country have ever won.

He was of singular uprightness and purity of character, alike in public and private life; a citizen who loved peace, he did his duty faithfully and well for four years of war when the honor of the nation called him to arms.

As congressman, as governor of his State, and finally as President, he rose to the foremost place among our statesmen, reaching a position that would satisfy the keenest ambition, but never lost that simple and thoughtful kindness toward every human being, great or small.

He grappled with more serious and complex problems than any President since Abraham Lincoln, etc., etc.

In the course of his speech Roosevelt emphasized his views on the necessity of judging men regardless of their wealth or poverty.

He referred to the dishonest rich man. The crowd cheered. Roosevelt stopped abruptly and, putting down his manuscript, said: "Wait a moment. I don't want you to applaud this last part unless you are willing to applaud the part I read first, to which you listened in silence. I want you to understand that I will stand just as straight for the rights of the honest man who wins his fortune by honest methods as I stand against the dishonest man who wins his fortune by dishonest methods."

His hearers applauded with cheers and hand-claps. He said: "Thank you! I will now proceed with my speech."

Roosevelt went from Canton direct to Keokuk, Iowa, to the opening of the great electric-power plant at the Keokuk dam in the Mississippi River.

He was joined by twenty-three governors interested in deep waterways and other conservation projects. They accompanied him to St. Louis, Cairo, and Memphis by boat.

At Memphis the governors left him, and he went into the Louisiana cane-brakes to hunt bear. He was the guest of Civil Service Commissioner McIl-lehany and John M. Parker, of New Orleans.

The President spent fifteen days in the cane-brakes. October 18 he killed a big black bear. The party shot three bear, six deer, one wild turkey, a dozen squirrels, one duck, one opossum, and one wildcat.

Roosevelt said they ate everything but the wild-cat, and there were times when they could have eaten the cat.

The President returned to Washington bronzed and feeling "bully," after a three and a half weeks' trip.

XXXV

ROOSEVELT CHOOSES TAFT AS HIS SUCCESSOR

A PREVIOUS chapter tells of Roosevelt on the train going to Mrs. McKinley's funeral as saying if he had the power of a dictator he would appoint Elihu Root President, and Secretary of War Taft as Chief Justice of the Supreme Court.

In talking with him later he said: "Root would make the best President, but Taft the best candidate."

Early in January, 1908, I received an invitation to be his guest in the White House for a few days.

The day of my arrival we dined at 8 o'clock. Those at the table were, as I remember now, the President and Mrs. Roosevelt, Secretary of War Taft and Mrs. Taft, Miss Mabel Boardman, General Francis Vinton Greene, and myself.

After dinner we went into the library on the second floor. Roosevelt, reclining in an easy chair, threw his head back, closed his eyes, and said: "I am the seventh son of a seventh daughter. I have clairvoyant powers. I see a man standing before me weighing about 350 pounds. There is something hanging over his head. I cannot make out what it is; it is hanging by a slender thread. At one time it looks like the Presidency—then again it looks like the Chief Justiceship."

"Make it the Presidency," exclaimed Mrs. Taft.

"Make it the Chief Justiceship," cried Mr. Taft.

Mrs. Taft had her wish. When the whirling plummet of President Roosevelt's vision came to rest over Mr. Taft's head it presented the Presidency side to the world.

President Harding in 1921 caused the same plummet to whirl again, and for the second time to rest above Mr. Taft's head. This time the face it presented was labelled "Chief Justiceship."

For the first time in history the two greatest offices in the gift of the American people have been bestowed upon the same man, and he a man in every way worthy to receive them.

After the guests had said "good night" the President and I went into his study, which for many years was the old cabinet room. We talked until very late.

I retired and spent an almost sleepless night in a high-ceilinged bedroom. My thoughts were of the history those four walls contained; especially my mind dwelt on Lincoln. I wondered if that greatest of all Americans had ever slept in that room.

I recalled a story told me by my old friend James W. Scott, of the Chicago *Herald*, in 1894. He said:

"My father took me to Washington in 1863 when I was a small boy. We arrived at night and went to a hotel—I think it was called the National Hotel. I could hardly go to sleep thinking of what I was to see the next day. After a restless night I awoke about 5.30 the next morning. My father was still asleep. So I quietly dressed and went down-stairs; a sleepy bell-boy told me how to reach the White House.

"As I looked through the high iron fence which surrounds the historic home of the Presidents, I saw a tall figure come out of the front door. From his pictures I knew it was Abraham Lincoln. He crossed the lawn to the gate leading to the War Office. I ran around to be near the gate when he came out.

"The President wore old-fashioned carpet slippers. His hands were clasped behind his back, his head down. As he came to where I stood he looked at me with the saddest pair of eyes I ever saw in a human being, and said: 'Good morning, Bub.'

"I was told that he went to the War Office at 6 o'clock in the morning to get the latest news from the front."

XXXVI

TAFT'S NOMINATION AND ELECTION, 1908

PRESIDENT ROOSEVELT'S pre-convention work for Secretary of War Taft was active up to the day of his nomination, June 18, 1908, in Chicago.

Taft was nominated on the first and only ballot taken. Bryan was again and for the third time the Democratic nominee for the Presidency.

Taft was elected November 2, 1908, receiving 321 electoral votes to Bryan's 162. With the exception of Roosevelt's plurality of about 2,545,500 in 1904, Taft received the largest plurality that any President had ever received, some 1,269,800 votes.

Mr. Taft arrived in Washington early in November, 1908, to close up some of his War Department duties. He had resigned June 30, but had some loose ends to adjust.

I called on President Roosevelt the end of November. He saw me in the cabinet-room waiting for the French ambassador to finish his audience. As the ambassador left, Roosevelt cried out:

"Oh, H. H., come here, I want to show you something.

"This morning as I read my Bible I came across

these verses in Ecclesiastes. I got a small Bible. marked them, and sent the Bible to Will Taft."

Solomon said in 2d chapter Ecclesiastes, 17th, 18th and 19th verses:

Therefore I hated life because the work that is wrought under the sun is grievous unto me: for all is vanity and vexation of spirit——

Yes—I hated all my labour which I had taken under the sun—because I shall leave it unto the man that shall be after me.

And who knoweth whether he shall be a wise man or a fool, yet shall he have rule over all my labour—wherein I have laboured and wherein I have shewed myself wise under the sun. This is also vanity.

XXXVII

THE TAFT–ROOSEVELT FIGHT FOR THE PRESIDENCY IN 1912

THE rift in the relations between President Taft and ex-President Roosevelt was apparent when Mr. Taft finished his inaugural address March 4, 1908.

Close observers wondered why Roosevelt broke all precedent by going to the Pennsylvania depot direct from the Senate chamber instead of riding back to the White House and receiving along with Taft the plaudits and cheers of the spectators who braved the blizzard to cheer the incoming and outgoing President.

I remember one of the Chicago *Record-Herald* staff saying it may have been cold outside, but Theodore must have been hot inside about something to forego the cheers of Pennsylvania Avenue.

The report that he was in a hurry to sail for Africa hardly held water, as a half or three-quarters of an hour delay in reaching New York would make little difference in his plans. He could have taken the next train, as they run hourly between Washington and New York.

When a new President takes the helm he is beset by office-seekers and their congressional backers.

For each one who goes away with a certificate of office ten are disappointed and unhappy. They form a Knocker's Union, and manage to find flaws in every act of the new executive. They organize "to get square" at the next election.

Mr. Taft had more than his allotted share of disgruntled politicians looking for his scalp. To some extent he was to blame, as he was rather too good-natured, and held out hopes that were doomed to disappointment.

Many of these men camped on his trail and threw their strength to Colonel Roosevelt, always a popular figure with a big following. He was especially strong with the young men just coming to manhood eager to cast their first vote for the red-blooded Roosevelt.

Did you ever know a young fellow whose pulse did not beat faster when he read of exploits with the gun? Roosevelt would be his hero and idol.

Almost any man who can gather 1,000 enthusiastic young men who believe in his sincerity, and scattered throughout the forty-eight States, can be nominated for the Presidency if he has the quality of leadership, and Roosevelt had that to a marked degree. Tens of thousands of young men were ready to follow him anywhere.

Early in 1912 he told me he had "a vault full of letters from young fellows anxious to have him run for the Presidency."

Colonel Roosevelt was fortunate in having several devoted followers who loved him from their hearts to their pocketbooks. Conspicuous among them were Frank A. Munsey, with a full purse and a string of newspapers and magazines; George W. Perkins, full of energy, resourcefulness, and the fruitful effect of a Morgan partnership; and Gifford Pinchot, fortunate in his choice of relatives.

None of them was in love with President Taft. They plead with Roosevelt to announce himself a candidate for the regular Republican nomination in June. He was reluctant to do so, as will be seen in his letter of January 16, 1912, to Mr. Munsey.

Senator La Follette was in the field for the nomination with several Western States backing him, but collapsed physically while delivering a speech in Philadelphia, February 2, 1912, putting him out of the running definitely. Many of his followers turned to Roosevelt, giving him a big lead in opposition to Taft.

A part of Colonel Roosevelt's letter of January 16, 1912, to Mr. Munsey appeared in the Chicago *Evening Post*. I wrote him as follows:

January 31, 1912.

MY DEAR FRIEND:

The Chicago *Evening Post* article was taken from a letter in the hands of Governor Osborn of Michigan, given to Mr. Shaffer and put out as if it came from New York. Osborn says you sent him a copy of a letter written to Frank Munsey—don't give me away, as it might hit a "working newspaper" man.

I am afraid you are drifting on a dangerous rock, my dear friend. The first thing you know your name will be used at the primaries and there will be an active fight for delegates between you and Taft. The La Follette people are sore to the bone because of the shift to you, and your position of acceptance "if the people demand it."

I know you don't want the nomination, but something must be done to keep from smashing everything in sight.

Do you remember the Hanna episode of eight years ago this month—how all the disappointed office-seekers and notoriety-seekers said you were a failure and could not be elected?

Now, I love your little finger more than Taft's 350 pounds but it seems to me that these people are putting you in a position of unfairness.

You see I am still "the brutal friend."

Yours faithfully,   H. H. KOHLSAAT.

Honorable Theodore Roosevelt,
The Outlook,
New York City.

February 5 he replied as follows:

"THE OUTLOOK"
287 FOURTH AVENUE
NEW YORK

Office of
Theodore Roosevelt

February 5th, 1912.

DEAR H. H.:

You are always a friend, you are not brutal, and I want you to speak frankly; but as to this question, I do not agree with you. I was very indignant that that letter was made public. In it, however, I stated my full and exact position. I am not in the least concerned with whether either Taft or La Follette is sore, and honestly I am not giving one thought to my own interests in the matter. I am trying to look at it purely from the public standpoint. Have you seen all the letter? If not, I will send it to you.

Faithfully yours,
(Signed) THEODORE ROOSEVELT.

H. H. Kohlsaat, Esq.,
The Chicago *Record-Herald*,
Chicago, Ill.

I wrote him asking for the entire Munsey letter, and received it from the colonel mailed from New York, February 14, 1912; he wrote:

DEAR H. H.: February 13, 1912.

Here is the letter. It is evident I have got to make a public statement soon.

Faithfully yours,

H. H. Kohlsaat, Esq., T. R.
Chicago.

MY DEAR MR. MUNSEY: January 16, 1912

I have received your long and cordial letter, together with the editorial. Permit me in the first place to thank you very warmly for the editorial. It seems to me that in the editorial you have stated the case exactly; so exactly, my dear Mr. Munsey, that to my mind it in itself furnishes the answer to the request you make that I should openly announce that if nominated I would not refuse the nomination. Your great kindness, and the disinterested friendliness of your action, entitle you to receive from me in full a statement of the reasons why

T^{he} Outlook

287 Fourth Avenue
New York

Office of
Theodore Roosevelt

February 5th, 1912.

Dear H. H.:

You are always a friend, you are not brutal, and I want
you to speak frankly; but as to this question, I do not ~~much~~
agree with you. I was very indignant that that letter was made
public. In it, however, I stated my full and exact position.
I am not in the least concerned with whether either Taft or
La Follette is sore, and honestly I am not giving one thought
to my own interests in the matter. I am trying to look at it
purely from the public standpoint. Have you seen all the
letter? If not, I will send it to you.

Faithfully yours,

Theodore Roosevelt

H. H. Kohlsaat, Esq.,
    The Chicago Record-Herald,
        Chicago, Ill.

I do not feel that, at the present time, it would be wise or proper for me to make any such statement. What the needs of the future may demand I cannot tell.

You say that my keeping silence leads to misconstruction, and gives opportunity for my enemies to make every kind of false statement about me, and to create in the minds of the people a false impression of me; some good people being led by my silence into the belief that it is useless to try to nominate me because I would certainly refuse, and others being misled into the belief that I am underhandedly intriguing for what I dare not openly ask; so that the impression on the public is detrimental to me.

My dear Sir, I entirely agree with you as to the fact that my silence is deliberately misrepresented by my enemies, with the purpose of confusing good people and getting them to take a wrong view; and moreover I entirely agree with you that this purpose is at least partly achieved. The trouble is that, as so often happens, this is a case where any course pursued would lead to just such misrepresentation, just such misjudgment, just such puzzling of the minds of good people. Personally, I think that any other course than the one I am adopting would at present lead to even more misrepresentation and misjudgment than actually exist. As I have again and again said, I am delighted to state my position fully and frankly, not only to any sincere and honest supporter, but to any sincere and honest opponent. What I have said to you, and am about to say to you, I have, for instance, said not only to other friends who think I ought to be nominated, but to friends (and even foes) who think I ought not to be nominated, provided only I could trust their sincerity, intelligence and truthfulness. For instance, I have said the same things to Secretary Stimson, Secretary Meyer and Congressman Longworth, who are supporting Taft; to Mr. Pinchot and Congressman Lenroot and Kent, who are supporting La Follette. I have said them to editors like Mr. Nelson, Mr. Van Walkenburg and Mr. Wright; I practically said them to the entire Aldine Club,—Democrats, Republicans, every one. I am not and shall not be a candidate. I shall not seek the nomination, nor would I accept it if it came to me as the result of an intrigue. But I will not tie my hands by a statement which would make it difficult or impossible for me to serve the public by undertaking a great task if the people as a whole seemed definitely to come to the conclusion that I ought to do that task. In other words, as far as in me lies I am endeavoring to look at this matter purely from the standpoint of the public interest, of the interest of the people as a whole, and not in the least from my own standpoint.

If I should consult only my own pleasure and interest, I should most emphatically and immediately announce that I would under no circumstances run. I have had all the honor that any man can have from holding the office of President. From every personal standpoint there is nothing for me to gain either in running for the office or in holding the office once more, and there is very much to lose. If, as I deem probable, Mr. Taft is nominated, and my name continues to be mentioned, my opponents will all say that I secretly or openly strove for the nomination and was defeated. If Mr. La Follette is nominated, the same thing will be said. If the utterly unexpected happens and I am nominated, I may very probably be defeated, in which case I shall be not only assailed but derided. If I won, I should take office carrying a burden for which I am not responsible, and facing conditions such as to make it almost certain, not only that I should not be able to accomplish all that I would like to accomplish, but that I should be very severely condemned, probably by a considerable majority of the people, for failure to accomplish what it would probably be beyond the power of any human being to accomplish.

Under such circumstances, if I consulted only my own interest, the obvious thing to do would be to announce that I would not obey any popular mandate, that I would not run if nominated. I shall not follow this course, because I am sincerely endeavoring to look at the matter only from the standpoint of the popular interest. It is not only necessary for the people to have the right instrument, the right tool, with which to work in any given emergency, but it is necessary that they themselves shall choose, and shall believe in the sufficiency of, that instrument. If at this particular crisis, with the particular problems ahead of us at this particular time, the people feel that I am the one man in sight to do the job, then I should regard myself as shirking a plain duty if I refused to do it. What I am interested in, remember, is not in the least holding the office, but doing a job that is actually worth doing; this is the position that to the best of my belief I have always taken, and always shall take. If the people should feel that I was the instrument to be used at this time, I should accept even although I knew that I should be broken and cast aside in the using; for often it is true that at a given moment there is one tool, one instrument, particularly available, and then that instrument must be used even though to use it necessarily means to break it. The right motto for any man is "Spend and be spent"; and if, in order to do a job worth doing from the public standpoint, he must pay with his own life, actual life on the field of battle, or political life in civic affairs, he must not grudge the payment. In short, I am not concerned with the welfare of any one man in this matter, not with Mr. Taft's welfare, nor Mr. La Follette's, and least of all with my own; I am concerned only with the welfare of the people of the United States.

Now your point is that when I feel thus I ought to be willing to state openly what I feel instead of answering, as I have hitherto answered to those who have asked me whether I would accept if nominated, that in the words of Abraham Lincoln I was not required to cross that bridge until I came to it. The reason is that in making any statement it is not only necessary to consider what the man actually means and actually says, and will be understood as saying by people who intelligently accept his statement at its face value, but also to consider what the statement will be held to mean by the great mass of people who are obliged to get their information more or less at second hand, and largely through instrumentalities like most of the New York dailies, such as *The American*, *The World*, *The Evening Post* and *The Times*, that is, through people who make their livelihood by the practice of slanderous mendacity for hire, and whose one purpose, as far as I am concerned, is to invent falsehood and to distort truth. If at this time I announced that I would accept if nominated, it would be blazoned abroad by all my enemies, and ultimately believed by a large portion even of my good friends and well wishers, that I had in my own interest so announced my candidacy, that I was an active candidate, that I was striving by every means to secure the nomination for President. At this time—whatever may be the case in the future—I do not see that any other outcome could be expected. It is simply a case where the language would not be accepted at its exact face value, and would inevitably be given a false construction; and this being so it seems to be wise not to use the language. Let me illustrate what I mean by referring you to the language in which after the election of 1904 I announced that I would not be a candidate for renomination. At the time, good friends of mine suggested that I should use some such formula as stating that I would not be a candidate in 1908 because of the custom that had grown up not to elect a man as President for a third consecutive term; but on thinking it over I became convinced that if I used such language it would inevitably be taken as an announcement that I would be a candidate for another term in 1912—and this in spite of the fact that of course the language if taken literally would only have referred to 1908, and have had no more bearing on 1912 than on 1916 or 1948. Accordingly I used language which simply stated that I paid heed to the essence and not the form of the wise custom of our forefathers in reference to the third term; the essence, of course, being that the custom applied just as much when my first term was the filling out of an unexpired term of my predecessor as if it had been an elective term, and that on the other hand it had no application whatever to the candidacy of a man who was not at the time in office, whether he had or had not been President before. Yet, even as it was, men at once began to ask me whether my refusal was to be held to apply to 1912 or to 1916; to which I of course responded that it would be preposterous to answer any such question one way or the other. By the way, I may recall to you that the very papers which are now howling to have me make some public statement are the ones which four and five years ago when I had made a definite public statement were continually howling I should make some additional statement. These people, people such as the editors of the newspapers above referred to, are not honest; they do not wish the truth, and to pay any heed to their demands would be worse than folly. If at present I said what you think I ought to say, they would merely substitute a worse set of misstatements for the set to which they are now giving currency.

Now, my dear Sir, as to what you say as to the desirability, no matter what the result, of my being "frank" and telling the whole public what I feel without any regard to whether or not it can be misrepresented.   Let me refer you to Lincoln.   Surely there was never a more straightforward nor a more sincere man than Lincoln, nor a man who more unhesitatingly, whenever the fit occasion arose, took the public fully and freely into his entire confidence.   But he consistently declined to make statements which though true would give opportunities for misrepresentation.   He sometimes made denials of false and slanderous accusations, when he deemed it necessary; but again and again he refused to do so when he thought that the denial would merely do additional harm.   Take the first volume of the Speeches, Letters and State Papers of Lincoln, edited by Hay and Nicolay, and turn to pages 633, 638, 646, 647, 651, 652 and 653.   When accused of having accepted money for a political speech, he wrote frankly to a correspondent who made inquiry, stating exactly what had happened, but adding, "I have made this explanation to you as a friend; but I wish no explanation made to our enemies.   What they want is a squabble and a fuss, and that they can have if we explain; and they cannot have it if we don't."   Later, when nominated, he received, as he says in a general letter signed by Nicolay answering them, a large number of letters asking that he declare his opinions on certain political points, and a large number of letters beseeching him to write nothing upon those political points; and to all alike he answered that his position had already been taken, and that he had nothing to add to or take from it. Again, when he was asked to deny the statements that he had been in a Know-Nothing Lodge, he wrote confidentially to his correspondent saying that the allegation was false, but adding, "Now a word of caution.   Our adversaries think they could gain a point if they could force me openly to deny the charge, by which some offense would be given to the Americans. For this reason it must not publicly appear that I am paying any attention to the charge." Again and again he thus answers letters privately and confidentially, stating his position, but requesting that it be not published for reasons similar to those just given. In one of his letters he says in reference to the suggestion that he make public some disclaimer, that he does not intend to do so because in his judgment it would do no good, adding, "Those who will not read or heed what I have already publicly said would not read or heed a repetition of it. If they heed not Moses and the Prophets, neither would they be persuaded though one rose from the dead." And again, when asked to make another public statement which it was hoped would have a good effect upon certain good men, he responded that as regards such good men he would have no objection to repeating what he had said seventy and seven times, and then added, (I condense) "But I have had men to deal with, both North and South, who are eager for something new upon which to base new misrepresentations. They would seize upon almost any letter I could write as being an awful coming down. I intend to not unnecessarily put any weapons in their hands."

Now, my dear Sir, it seems to me that the homely commonsense with which Lincoln spoke, in these letters which I have quoted, can be applied now. Nothing I could say, no statement or explanation by me, would avail to prevent deliberate misrepresentation by bad men, designed to puzzle and mislead good men, who, from the nature of the case, could not be expected to have firsthand information. They now misrepresent my position designedly and purposefully. They would merely misrepresent it even more effectively if I should at this time

make the statement you desire. It may be that in the
end it will be necessary to make such a statement, or
some other public statement; but the time is not now.
I am well aware of the disadvantage of not making such
a statement, but I think the disadvantage of making it
would be greater. The position is a hard one. It is hard
for me; it is some ways harder for disinterested men like
yourself who believe that I could do service as President,
and who naturally feel indignant that I do not come forward in a way which as they think would enable them to
to make me President, (and of course the fact that I do
not make it amply warrants you, and all who think as
you do, in at any time supporting any other man instead
of me.)

If my position were only a pose, I should certainly
act differently from the way I am acting, for I am well
aware that the way I am acting is not the way in which
to act if I desire to be made President. But my attitude
is not a pose, I am acting as I do because, according to
my lights, I am endeavoring, in not a too easy position,
to do what I believe the interests of the people demand.
From this standpoint I am convinced that although it is
entirely proper for other men to seek the Presidency, it
is neither wise nor proper for me to do so, the conditions
being what they actually are. I have been President; I
was President for nearly eight years; I am well known
to the American people; I am to be judged not by words
but by my acts; and whether the people like or dislike
me, they have these acts all before them for their decision—and nobody, my dear Sir, has helped more than
you have helped to put these acts clearly before them.
My usefulness in the Presidency as conditions now are
would depend not merely upon the people wishing me to
be President, but upon their having good reason to believe that I was President because of their wishes, because

of their desire that I should do a given job, which they felt I could do better than any one else, and not because of any personal ambition on my part. Even if I got the Presidency, as a result of what might seem to be active effort on my part to get it for my own sake, the mere fact of having thus obtained it would I fear prevent my being of use to the people in the office. Under these circumstances I must not put myself in a position which would look as if I were seeking the office, as if I were trying to get it for my own sake. I know well that this means in all probability some one else will be nominated and elected; for where others actively seek the nomination, their friends as is natural actively work for them, and give the skilful direction and leadership without which even a strongly aroused public opinion generally fails to find expression. Therefore I have all along felt that even if there should be a strong popular demand for me (as to which I can pass no judgment) yet that unless this demand were literally overwhelming it could hardly make itself effective. But it seems to me that it is better that it should not make itself effective rather than that by any action of mine I should make it seem that I desire the Presidency for my own sake, or am willing to accept it unless it comes to me as the result of a real popular movement, giving expression to a demand from at least a substantial portion of the plain people that I should undertake a given task in the interest of the people as a whole. Before I speak there should be some tangible evidence that such is the case.

With very high regard,

Faithfully yours,

(Signed) THEODORE ROOSEVELT.

Mr. Frank A. Munsey
175 Fifth Avenue,
New York City

The governors of seven States soon after this united in an appeal to Roosevelt to announce his candidacy. They were Governor Bass, of New Hampshire, Governor Hadley, of Missouri, Governor Osborn, of Michigan, Governor Glasscock, of West Virginia, Governor Carey, of Wyoming, Governor Aldrich, of Nebraska, and Governor Stubbs, of Kansas.

The appeal had its effect. Colonel Roosevelt "threw his hat into the ring" February 26, 1912, and from that day until the end of the June convention was an active candidate against President Taft.

The Record-Herald published several editorials begging Colonel Roosevelt not to enter the field against Taft, as I felt he could not win the nomination. The Republican organization of the country was against him, and his candidacy, unless successful in June, surely meant two Republican candidates against one Democrat, and the Democrats would win, no matter who they nominated.

The Roosevelt adherents were so bitter against Taft, and were so sure of Roosevelt's great popularity, I was strong in the belief they would form a new party.

As to my own position I received the following letter from my good friend George E. Roberts, director of the mint:

TREASURY DEPARTMENT
OFFICE OF DIRECTOR OF THE MINT
WASHINGTON

MY DEAR MR. KOHLSAAT: March 2, 1912.

I cannot forbear expressing my gratification over the position taken by *The Record-Herald*. I know, of course, what your relations with Colonel Roosevelt have been, and your sincere regard and friendship for him. I know it was not an easy matter for you to take the stand you have assumed but I am sure that all your friends will honor you for it. I most deeply regret Colonel Roosevelt's action for I cannot see anything to be gained by it for any cause he has at heart.

Sincerely yours,
(Signed) GEO. E. ROBERTS.

Mr. H. H. Kohlsaat,
Editor, Chicago *Record-Herald*,
Chicago, Ill.

I also received the following letter from President Taft:

THE WHITE HOUSE
WASHINGTON

MY DEAR MR. KOHLSAAT,   March 4, 1912

I write to thank you for your support at a time when the strongest personal considerations would move you to come out for Colonel Roosevelt.

I know that it is your patriotic sense of duty and love of our admirable and tried form of government that prompts you but I feel that I ought gratefully to acknowledge it at any rate.

I had the pleasure of entertaining Mr. Rosenwald last

week and enabling him to dream of the shades of former presidents under the White House roof.

With best wishes,

Sincerely yours,   WM. H. TAFT.

H. H. Kohlsaat, Esq.,
The Record-Herald, Chicago, Ill.

P. S.   A year hence what?

March 15, 1912, I wrote Colonel Roosevelt the following letter, which he never answered. All correspondence between us ceased until 1918.

March 15, 1912.

MY DEAR FRIEND:

In writing this I want you to know that it is written with affectionate regard and no personal interest in the coming election.

Mr. Taft can give me nothing, I want no office for myself nor friends—this was my attitude under McKinley and also when you were in the White House. So, if I am brutally frank you know it is not self interest.

I am greatly distressed about your future. It seems to me you have no show of nomination and will find yourself in the position of trying to reach the Presidency and failing. If you look over the field without prejudice how can you figure out votes enough to nominate! I can't see any possible chance.

As to "not caring whether you win or not" it is a question of "principles not office" that you are striving for— you can do more in your present position to bring about those principles than you could to attempt to reach the Presidency and fail.

The men who have been talking to you, especially the seven little governors, are trying to ride into office on your coat tails. They *do* care whether "they win or not."

There is no question of your popularity with the masses, but you are stronger in the background as a possibility than you are as an out and out candidate.

There is a great change taking place throughout the Middle West since your Columbus speech. There is no sympathy whatever with "the recall of judicial decisions," the "anti third term" sentiment is strong, and the feeling that it is unfair to Taft is growing.

You absolutely forced Taft on the ticket. You talked to me like a "Dutch Uncle" because I did not "cotton" to him. He did not make good the first two years but has found himself and is giving satisfaction. He arouses no enthusiasm, but the universal sentiment is that he is sincere.

You have no "pride of opinion." You are the most courageous man I ever met in reversing your opinion or position if you were convinced you were doing right by doing so. Let me entreat you to reconsider your decision to be a candidate and withdraw now, before the majority of delegates are chosen.

I write this as a true friend who has nothing but your personal welfare at heart. I hate to see you dragged into an unseemly struggle to pull other people's chestnuts out of the fire.

As ever, faithfully yours,

(Signed) H. H. KOHLSAAT.

Honorable Theodore Roosevelt,
The Outlook, New York City.

P. S. When people say that Taft cannot be re-elected they do not know what they are talking about. Within the last two weeks forces have been lined up for Taft which are not good in the primaries but all powerful in elections. I know whereof I speak.

XXXVIII

THE BREAK BETWEEN ROOSEVELT
AND TAFT

In August, 1911, I received a note from Colonel
Roosevelt asking me to wire him on leaving Chicago
for New York. He wanted me to lunch with him
in *The Outlook* office and meet his associates.

I did as requested and found a message at the
Holland House on my arrival inviting me to lunch
the next day, which was a Friday. As I remember,
the colonel told me it was the first luncheon they
had served in *The Outlook* office.

After the meal we went into his room. He told
his secretary, Mr. Harper, not to ring his telephone
or knock on the door until he opened it.

We at once plunged into the subject of the in-
creasing coolness between President Taft and himself. I asked him what was the cause of the apparent
break in their relations.

The colonel said when Taft was elected in 1908
he came to Washington to gather up some loose
ends in the War Department, from which he resigned
as Secretary of War, June 30, 1908. He said more

than half of Loeb's time was taken by people calling, writing, or telephoning for an appointment with Taft. He said senators and congressmen dropped him completely and hunted for Taft. They paid no attention to him and took no interest in bills he was anxious to have passed before the end of his term.

I told him that was human nature. "The King is dead. Long live the King," applied to presidents as well as kings.

He continued: "When I was leaving for Africa, Taft sent Archie Butt to the boat to say he felt very grateful to me for doing what I did to make him President. He said he owed his nomination and election to the Presidency to me and his brother Charley. I sent back word that 'his brother Charley gave him money, but I gave him the Presidency.'"

The colonel continued: "I was very anxious to have 'Jimmie' Garfield and Oscar Straus retained in the cabinet, Garfield to carry out my policies, especially the conservation policies. Taft promised me he would appoint them, and they went ahead with their plans to remain in the cabinet, but were very much surprised a short time before Inauguration, March 4, 1909, to be told he had decided to appoint men of his own selection."

After Roosevelt recited some inconsequential annoyances, I said: "Do you know you have not given one good, valid reason for breaking with your old friend Taft? You forced his nomination on the country and should be the last to desert him." I continued: "I'll tell you what is the trouble. You foolishly issued a statement the night of your election in 1904, saying you would not be a candidate in 1908 for what you called a 'third term,' which was not a third term, as you were serving out McKinley's second term. You could have been renominated easily if it had not been for that declaration. You then chose Taft to be your successor, expecting him to look to you for advice and guidance. Naturally, he wanted to be President on his own hook, and appoint a cabinet of his own choosing."

Roosevelt screwed up his mouth and said: "I would cut that hand right off there," putting his finger on his wrist, "if I could have recalled that statement given to the Associated Press."

Without telling Roosevelt I was going to Washington, I took the Congressional Limited that afternoon.

I had promised my friend Cyrus H. McCormick to try to arrange an interview in the White House some evening between President Taft, Mr. McCormick, John P. Wilson, and Edgar A. Bancroft, of the International Harvester Company, with the

Attorney-General, George W. Wickersham, present; so I called on President Taft the next day about noon.

After arranging a date for an evening meeting the President said: "Have you a luncheon engagement? If not, come back at one-thirty; only Mrs. Taft and some of the school friends of the children will be present."

After luncheon the President led the way to the White House porch and said: "I want to have a frank talk with you." In substance he said: "You are a great friend of Colonel Roosevelt's. Through some misunderstanding he feels hurt with me. I must have done something that displeased him very much. Knowingly I have never done anything to hurt his feelings. I may have been tactless, but not intentionally would I do anything to displease him. I owe him everything. He is responsible for my being President. I am so distressed it keeps me awake nights."

The President showed considerable emotion. His eyes filled with tears. I said: "Perhaps when you sent Archie Butt to the boat when the colonel went to Africa with the message that he, the colonel, and your brother Charley made you President, it irritated him." Taft replied: "But I didn't send any such message!" "Or," I said, "your failure to appoint Garfield and Straus to cabinet positions, as you promised Roosevelt, made him mad!" "But I didn't promise to appoint them!" answered Taft. "I don't know where you get your information, but you are entirely wrong!"

I did not tell him of my visit with Colonel Roosevelt the day before, but replied: "The newspapers have printed numerous stories to that effect." The President said: "What time does your train go?" I told him "Three-forty," as I remember. "Come down-stairs to my office and I will show you all the correspondence between Roosevelt and myself since the election of 1908 to date."

On entering the office, Taft asked his secretary, Charles D. Hilles, to bring him all the correspondence that had passed between Colonel Roosevelt and himself since the election.

I read all of the original Roosevelt letters and copies of Taft's to Roosevelt. Colonel Roosevelt's letters were so at variance with what he told me the day before, I was dumfounded, and asked Taft if he would give me copies of them. He called Mr. Hilles in and had him make copies and send to me at Chicago. He also gave me a copy of a letter he had written his brother Horace giving his reasons for signing the Payne-Aldrich Tariff Bill.

After the publication in *The Saturday Evening Post* of the letter to Horace Taft, the Chief Justice requested that the Roosevelt-Taft letters be held by

From a photograph, copyright, 1922, by Harris and Ewing

PRESIDENT TAFT

Now Chief Justice Taft, reading a telegram announcing the birth of a second grandson within
twenty-four hours

his family and not published until after his death. May it be many years before they are made public.

I have never been able to explain to my satisfaction why Colonel Roosevelt told me the story of Archie Butt's coming to the steamer, as he left for Africa, with a message from President Taft. But he *did* tell me the incident as I relate it.

His warm friend and coeditor of *The Outlook*, Mr. Lawrence F. Abbott, told me some few weeks ago in the Century Club, New York, he was positive no such message was received by Colonel Roosevelt from President Taft.

As to the promise to retain Garfield and Straus in his cabinet, Mr. Abbott, in his "Impressions of Theodore Roosevelt," says on page 67:

"Mr. Taft on his election no doubt wished to carry on the work of his predecessor, and if not publicly often privately said it was his desire and intention to retain those cabinet colleagues of Mr. Roosevelt who had contributed so much to the recreation of the Republican party." (*Note by Mr. Roosevelt :* 'He told me so, and authorized me to tell the cabinet, especially Garfield, Straus, and Luke Wright.')

Mr. Abbott continues:

"But this intention became gradually modified during the winter of 1908 and 1909. Only one member of the cabinet was retained, and the one member who was Mr. Roosevelt's most intimate associate, and on whom he depended more than on any one else in his struggle to take the government out of the control of 'Big Business,' the member of all others whom he would have preferred to see retained, was not retained. I refer, of course, to Mr. James Garfield, Mr. Roosevelt's Secretary of the Interior."

XXXIX

THE REPUBLICAN NATIONAL CONVENTION
OF 1912

THE Republican national convention of 1912 met
in the Coliseum in Chicago, June 18, 1912. Elihu
Root presided, as one writer described it, "without
loss of temper."

There was great friction over seating contested
delegates. Mr. Taft was finally renominated by
561 votes. Roosevelt received 107, La Follette, 41,
Cummins, of Iowa, 17, Charles E. Hughes, 2. Roosevelt delegates to the number of 344 did not vote, as
he requested them not to do so. Presumably many of
them came to the Progressive convention, August 5.

There was little life in the Taft campaign, a great
deal of enthusiasm in the Roosevelt organization,
and a positive feeling they would win in the Democratic camp. The vote in November verified their
confidence. Woodrow Wilson received 6,286,214;
Roosevelt, 4,126,020; Taft, 3,483,922, a total Republican vote of 7,609,942 against the 6,286,214
for Mr. Wilson, or a plurality of 1,323,728 for the
Republican and Progressive tickets.

When the Progressive party met in Chicago, August 5, 1912, Medill McCormick met Colonel Roose-

velt at the Lake Shore Railway depot and rode to the Congress Hotel. On the way he is reported to have said that only one paper in Chicago was bitterly against Colonel Roosevelt, and named *The Inter-Ocean*, which at that date, June, 1912, was owned and edited by Mr. George W. Hinman. Mr. McCormick told him crooked politicians owned the bonds of *The Inter-Ocean*, and named Senator William Lorimer as one of the bondholders.

When Roosevelt reached the hotel a great crowd greeted him and called for a speech. He stood up in the machine, and in the course of his speech said something to the effect that he was opposed in Chicago only by crooked newspapers whose bonds were owned by crooked politicians. "If you want to know who runs *The Record-Herald*, look up its bondholders." Mr. McCormick interrupted and said: "Not *The Record-Herald*, colonel, *The Inter-Ocean*." Roosevelt paid no heed to Mr. McCormick's interruption. After he had finished talking and gone into the hotel, the reporters of the Chicago papers went to his room and said: "You did not mean *The Record-Herald* bonds, colonel, did you? Mr. Kohlsaat has been your stanch friend for years." The colonel said: "What did I say?" "You said: 'If you want to know who runs *The Record-Herald*, look up its bondholders.'" He answered: "Well, if I said it, I'll stick to it."

PRESIDENT WILSON

The only paper in Chicago that printed that part of Colonel Roosevelt's speech was *The Record-Herald;* the other papers, without a single exception, ignored it, and I want to bear witness here to the honest, chivalrous treatment accorded me by my fellow publishers of Chicago. They knew Victor F. Lawson, of the Chicago *Daily News,* and I were the principal bondholders of *The Record-Herald,* and refused to publish the slander.

I was at the Chicago Golf Club in Wheaton when the managing editor of *The Record-Herald* telephoned me that part of Colonel Roosevelt's speech referring to the bonds. He asked if he could print it. I said: "Yes, publish exactly what he said; a lie finally kills itself."

Colonel Roosevelt told a mutual friend who is still living, "he thought Herman Kohlsaat would follow him to the death," and I would have done so if he had been fair; but he was not fair to President Taft, nor the Republican party, which lived to rue the day Colonel Roosevelt's ambition got the better of his judgment.

The Progressive convention met in Orchestra Hall, Chicago, August 5, 1912. There was great confusion and excitement. Colonel Roosevelt and Hiram Johnson, of California, were nominated for President and Vice-President.

I was not present, but a Chicago friend who was

told me some of the funny incidents which occurred. He said the band was playing with all the wind and muscle they could muster. The bass drummer seemed to have caught some of Colonel Roosevelt's "Big Stick" movements. In the midst of the hubbub Senator Beveridge appeared on the floor with his hair very much dishevelled as he cried out, "Where is that blankety-blank preacher, we want him to start his prayer." And my friend said: "To see good old Oscar Straus singing 'Onward, Christian Soldiers' with all his might was worth coming in from Lake Forest to see."

XL

LONDON'S FIRST ZEPPELIN RAID

I ARRIVED at the Victoria Hotel, London, September 7, 1915. My straw hat was a disreputable-looking piece of head-gear. As I started out to a dinner with the family of H. Gordon Selfridge, I asked the head porter, covered with gold buttons and braid, if he thought my hat would attract the attention of a "zepp." He replied very seriously: "I don't think so, sir—it would be 'ard to see your 'at from so 'igh up."

There had been much discussion in the newspapers of a probable raid on London; search-lights and guns had been installed on the roof of the War Office and other buildings in the city.

On my return from dinner, I retired about 11 o'clock, and was awakened by rapid-firing guns; I went to the window and saw two or three search-lights centred directly over my window on the top floor of the hotel. I could not see the zeppelin because of the overhanging roof. It passed on uninjured. I rang for the chambermaid to ask if any damage had been done by bombs after the ship passed the hotel, but could get no answer to my ring. Half or three quarters of an hour later she knocked on the door. When I asked why the bell was not answered, she said, "I was in the basement, sir," and then told me of a big fire to be seen from the front of the house toward St. Paul's Cathedral.

Next morning I asked the day chambermaid where she was when the "zepp" came. She replied: "I was in bed, sir, in the top of the 'ouse, sir. They pulled me out and made me walk down the cold stone steps in my bare feet to the basement." I said: "That is where the night maid told me she went. Why did no one call me to warn me of the danger?" She replied: "Oh, sir, you were not under the Employers' Liability Act." A few days later, with the aid of an intelligent taxicab driver and a friend, I drove over the district invaded by the "zepp." My friend estimated the damage at over $5,000,000, but every London newspaper said the damage was nominal, and printed simply a paragraph. The Associated Press carried over 2,000 words to the censor to be sent to the United States. He cut it, as I remember, to about sixty words.

My friend Sir Henry Truman Wood, secretary of the Society of Arts, London, gave me a visitor's card to the Athenæum Club.

He explained that visitors, as well as members, in order to be eligible, must have written a book or thesis before they were admitted inside the club doors. I said: "How in the world did I get in then?" He answered: "I wrote in the visitor's book you were the author of the Gold Plank, and they think that is a novel."

A few days later I wanted to go to Paris, and went to the French Consulate to get a passport; an official looked at my American passport, and when he came to my occupation, which read "newspaper publisher," he asked: "What department of the newspaper?" I replied: "Editor." He said: "Then you are a journalist." I replied: "Only very young reporters call themselves 'journalists' in America." But he insisted, so I let it go on the passport.

Next day I boarded the ill-fated *Sussex*. When we arrived at Dieppe we had to stand nearly two hours on the slippery seaweed-covered steps of the landing, and then pass before a half-dozen French officials. When they compared my American and French passports and saw me described as a "newspaper publisher" in the American and a "journalist" in the French, it created a mild panic. I do not understand French, but when a soldier took me by the arm and marched me down the quay, I saw a night in jail before me. When we reached a small building, I was shown into the presence of an official who spoke English indifferently, but well enough to impress me that I had committed some crime. He pointed his accusing finger at the discrepancy of occupation in the passports. I explained to him how it happened, but he was unconvinced, so I took a package of letters from my satchel that Myron T. Herrick had given me to friends of his in Paris. When he recognized Mr. Herrick's name, clicking his heels together and saluting me, he said, "Pardon, monsieur, pardon; a friend of Ambassador Herrick's is always welcome to France," and turning to a military aide instructed him to see that I had a good seat on the express for Paris, where I finally landed about 2 o'clock in the morning.

A few days later, with the kind assistance of our ambassador, William G. Sharp, General Joffre gave Colonel Cosby, our military attaché, and me a permit to go into the valley of the Marne for forty-eight hours. It was one week before the Champagne drive, and all visitors to that sector had been barred.

We left Paris in a motor early in the morning and got back about midnight. A week before they had celebrated the first anniversary of the battle of the Marne by decorating the graves of the French with flowers and flags and the Germans with green boughs. The French graves and trenches were surrounded by a little white picket fence, and the German by a fence painted black.

Many of the crosses at the head of the graves were covered with the caps of the poilu. I remarked to Colonel Cosby it would not be long before tourists carried away the caps. I hope no American would be guilty of such desecration.

When we left Senlis we passed men at work rebuilding the trenches and repairing the barbed-wire defenses, getting ready for another attack on Paris. The road was lined with poplar-trees, the tops shot off, leaving a bare trunk some ten or twelve feet high. At one of the crossroads we came to a weatherbeaten crucifix that had escaped injury by shot and shell. In the crown of thorns on the Saviour's head a bird had built her nest. We saw very few birds flying about. Colonel Cosby said the constant roar of cannon and aeroplanes had driven them away.

We passed an old woman on the road with heavy bundles on her head and in both hands. I asked the chauffeur to back up and give her a lift. She took us to a group of farm buildings about three miles away. The village consisted of some 125 inhabitants and a fourteenth-century church. The woman showed us a community compound, the buildings badly damaged by German shells. She said they lost over forty cows and a number of horses. Colonel Cosby asked her if she had men in the war. She said: "Yes, my husband and three sons; two of my boys were killed and one is in a French hospital, and my husband wounded and a prisoner in Germany." Through Colonel Cosby I said: "Losing your husband and sons, you have made great sacrifice for your country." She drew herself up defiantly and said: "I wish I had four more to fight for my beloved France."

As we turned toward Paris we called on Miss Mildred Aldrich, author of "A Hilltop on the Marne," to me the most human and interesting story of the war. Miss Aldrich lived on a crest near Meaux. It gave her a view of fifteen miles of battle front, September 7, 8, and 9, 1914. In the bright light of a full harvest-moon from her front door she described the battle scenes. In turn, she fed German, French, and English troops as they passed her home, formerly a peasant's cottage.

A few days later I returned to London. My friend John Lane, the publisher, arranged to have me lunch with Premier and Mrs. Asquith at 10 Downing Street. There were fourteen guests at the table. I sat next to Mrs. Asquith, and greatly enjoyed her bright remarks. Some people criticise her frankness, but no one can deny her brilliancy.

Mrs. Asquith severely criticised President Wilson for not getting into the war when Germany invaded Belgium. I tried to explain that Congress was the only body that could declare war. The President could propose but Congress did the disposing, and that this country was taken unawares by Germany's declaration of war.

It was rather difficult for me to talk, as the bird

on my plate had been dead a long time, and my Illinois birth did not train me to the English standard of a "high" bird. It was hard to control my mind and stomach at the same time.

As the guests were leaving, Mr. Asquith and I took a window-seat and discussed the war and the possible participation of America. I asked him how long the war would last. He said, pointing to a boy in the street: "Do you see that boy down there? He knows as much about it as I do." He then predicted the war would go on until Europe was exhausted—a prophecy that has come true.

I was asked if I would like to meet King George, and replied "I would rather meet the other George," so my friend Sydney Brooks arranged to have me lunch with Mr. Lloyd George, then Minister of Munitions, 11 Downing Street. The lunch-hour was set for 1 o'clock. We were delayed downstairs for a few minutes. When we reached the dining-room, Mr. Lloyd George had finished his lunch and was lighting a big fat cigar. He apologized and said he had an appointment with Mr. Thomas, French Minister of Munitions, in half an hour, and so had started his meal a quarter of an hour before we arrived. He told the waitress she need not remain and, closing the door, he passed the food from the sideboard to Mr. Brooks and me through two or three courses.

He asked many questions about American politics and politicians; the characteristics of the latter interested him greatly. I told him some of the anecdotes related in these recollections. He looked at his watch and said: "Good Lord, I am an hour late in my appointment with Thomas." After asking me to send him all the books and anecdotes I could find of Lincoln, he left us to go to his meeting.

I returned to the United States in November, and went again to France January 4, 1916, sailing on the *Rochambeau*, bound for Bordeaux. As we neared the mouth of the Garonne a bulletin was posted at noon forbidding the showing of any lights. Portholes were ordered covered; no cigars or cigarettes must be lighted on deck. Many passengers stayed up all night; the smoking-room was anti-Volstead. For two or three days we had been having boat drills; each passenger assigned to his or her particular seat in the life-boat. At night our life-preservers were spread out ready to be put on if attacked by a "sub." All these preparations accentuated the danger while passing through the "sub" zone.

One passenger went to his stateroom about 2 in the morning, and found his wife fully dressed sitting on a camp-stool. He said: "Why aren't you in your berth?" She replied: "I took a bath, put on the finest lingerie I possess and my very best dress. If this ship goes down, I don't propose to be picked up on the shores of France in an old nightgown." The eternal feminine running true to form.

Along about midnight I was leaning on the rail talking to a Mr. Spieden, of New York, a dealer in essential oils, on his way to Spain. He told me he was in Berlin at the Hotel Adlon in April 1915, where he met a Mr. Thomson of George H. McFadden & Brother, cotton brokers of Philadelphia. The United States had put an embargo on cotton to Germany, and Mr. Thomson was returning to New York. Some friends in Bremen gave him a farewell dinner and asked if a submarine captain could be invited. He consented. Next morning he arrived in Berlin and told Mr. Spieden the following story: "During the dinner I asked the captain to tell of the life of a submarine. He described how she submerged and lay on the bottom of the English Channel during the night and came up in the early morning to look for her prey. I asked him if when they came up some morning and only had one shell left they should see three ships—an English war-vessel, a merchantman laden with ammunition, and a passenger-ship carrying women and children—remembering he had only one shell, which ship he would take. To which he replied, that they would strike the passenger-ship, as that was the only way to strike terror to the English. I then asked him to go a step further and assume that the passenger-ship should be the *Lusitania*, which was known to carry a large number of men, women, and children from neutral countries. He replied: 'We have had orders for the last six weeks to get the *Lusitania*.' "

The *Lusitania* was sunk on the 7th of May, 1915, two or three weeks after the Thomson dinner. I venture the assertion that if the people of the United States had known of the German Government's order to "get the *Lusitania*," we should have entered the war in May, 1915, instead of April, 1917. The fiendish crime was thought to be the work of an irresponsible "sub" captain, a belief fostered by the German officials themselves.

From an entirely responsible source I received the following information of how the decision was reached to sink the *Lusitania:*

In February, 1915, four men met in Dressler's restaurant in Unter den Linden, Berlin. They were Admiral von Tirpitz, von Bethmann-Hollweg, Ballin, of the Hamburg-American Line, and von Riedemann, the Standard Oil magnate of Germany. Von Tirpitz insisted the only way to end the war was to sink not only the *Lusitania* but all ships, neutral as well as enemy, that America did not want to go to war and would insist on peace if American ships were to be attacked. Von Bethmann-Hollweg shrugged his shoulders and assumed a neutral attitude. Ballin and von Riedemann bitterly opposed the suggestion. Finally it was decided to put it up to two high personages. Von Tirpitz saw them, and later showed the other three the signatures of the Kaiser and von Falkenhayn approving the plan. Not long afterward von Riedemann disappeared from Germany. I am not sure whether he is dead or alive. Herr Ballin is supposed to have committed suicide.

The Kaiser abdicated at Spa when General Gröner, Ludendorff's successor, backed by Hindenburg, told him the troops would no longer follow him. His flight, November 9, 1918, into neutral Holland was undertaken absolutely of his own accord, without the knowledge of his General Staff or any of his officers.

This report of the Kaiser's flight, unknown to any of his officers, is confirmed in a cable to the New York *Times* dated September 11, 1922, which reads as follows:

Berlin, September 11.

The reactionary *Der Tag* tonight publishes a letter from Hindenburg to the ex-Kaiser, dated Hanover, July 28, obviously intended as a complete whitewash of the ex-Kaiser's flight to Holland. The letter is as follows:

Most Exalted, All Mightiest Kaiser, Most Gracious Kaiser, King and Lord!

For the decision which your Majesty made on the ill-fated November 9, based on the unanimous recommendation of all your competent advisers, I bear my share of responsibility. Grave danger threatened that your Majesty's person would be seized by mutineers and delivered into the hands of internal or external enemies. Such shame and disgrace had to be spared the fatherland under all circumstances.

For this reason, in making my report to your Majesty on the afternoon of the 9th in the name of us all, I recommended crossing over into Holland as a last extremity, a measure which, moreover, I considered merely as a temporary expedient. That I urged an immediate departure on the night of the 9th is an error which recently, against my will, was mentioned publicly.

For me there is no doubt that your Majesty would not have gone off if your all-highest self had not believed that I as Chief of the General Staff regarded this step as imperative in the interest of your Majesty and the fatherland. In the protocol of July 27, 1919, it is already stated that I received the news of your Majesty's departure only after it was completed.

In conclusion I beg to assure your Majesty most humbly that all my life long I have maintained and always will maintain unlimited loyalty to my Kaiser, King and Lord, and am therefore also willing always and everywhere to bear my full share of responsibility for the decision of November 9, 1918.

With the deepest awe and greatest thankfulness, I remain always your imperial and royal Majesty's alleruntertaenigster.

HINDENBURG.

The Kaiser's former officers detest him and charge him with cowardice in running away. The chances of his or the Crown Prince's ever coming back into power is beyond any reasonable conception.

I decided when we reached Bordeaux to cable the Thomson story to President Wilson, but feared the French officials would hold me to inquire how I got the information; so I left for Paris and saw Ambassador Sharp, and on his advice I waited until reaching London before sending it, January 26, 1916.

The day I sent it, Lady Cunard, in the home of the Honorable Mrs. Lionel Guest, daughter of our former Minister to France, John Bigelow, asked me to bring the cable to a dinner she was giving to the Premier and Mrs. Asquith that night. I did so. Mr. Balfour, and I think Lord Desborough, and several other gentlemen and their wives were present. After the ladies had left the table Mr. Asquith said Lady Cunard had told him that I had sent an important cable to President Wilson, and asked if he could see it. As he read it, Mr. Balfour looked over his shoulder and read it. The two men went into a corner of the room and conversed in low tones for a few minutes. Finally Mr. Asquith said: "That is a very important piece of information. What effect will it have on your government?" I replied: "If we had known it ten months earlier, we should probably have declared war when the *Lusitania* was torpedoed."

On the night of January 27, 1916, President Wilson delivered a ringing preparedness speech before the Railway Business Association at the Waldorf Hotel, New York. Mr. Tumulty told me the President received my cable before leaving Washington that morning. In the course of his speech, which he had given to the Associated Press early in the day, he said: "I cannot tell you what the international situation will be to-morrow, and I use the words literally, and I would not dare keep silent and let the country suppose that to-morrow was certain to be as bright as to-day." According to the London evening papers of the 28th, he departed from his manuscript, looked up and said in effect: "Gentlemen, if you could see the cables I am receiving, you would realize we were on the brink of war every day." The London papers printed Mr. Wilson's interpolation under two-column heads. It created a great sensation and was widely commented on. England and France were very anxious to see us get into the war at once, but I believe Mr. Wilson acted wisely in waiting for the sentiment of the country to back him up before going to Congress with a declaration of war.

THE BREACH BETWEEN ROOSEVELT AND KOHLSAAT

All correspondence between Colonel Roosevelt and myself had ceased after his attack on me from an automobile in front of the Congress Hotel in June, 1912. Mr. Munsey, George W. Perkins, and

March 12, 1918.

Dear H.H.

Three cheers for you! Now, when
you next come to New York you must let me know
and come out here to lunch or dinner. You
can bet I am going to act just along the lines
you advise in your letter.

Faithfully yours,

Theodore Roosevelt

Mr. H. H. Kohlsaat,
1440 First National Bank Bldg.,
Chicago, Ill.

other mutual friends had tried to patch up our differences, but I insisted the colonel apologize publicly for his unjust attack, which is told in a previous chapter, but nothing came of it.

June, 1917, the colonel came to Chicago. As I was leaving the Chicago Club after lunch I met my friend John T. McCutcheon and his wife on their way to the Congress Hotel to call on Roosevelt. McCutcheon said: "Come with us and I am sure the colonel will be glad to see you." I hesitated a moment and said: "All right, I will. The country is at war. No one knows what will happen. I am willing to meet the colonel half-way and forgive and forget the past." As we entered the large parlor we saw Roosevelt in his bedroom with his back to the door talking to Seth Bullock, of South Dakota, and James Garfield. When he entered the room to shake hands with some forty people waiting to see him, he caught sight of Mr. and Mrs. McCutcheon and me. He rushed to us, and after shaking hands with Mrs. McCutcheon he grabbed me by both hands and exclaimed: "By George, my wife and children will be glad I saw you." Still holding my hand with his left, he passed around the room shaking hands with his callers. Again he expressed his pleasure over our meeting; no reference was made to the five years of silence.

July 2 he wrote me the following letter:

OYSTER BAY

LONG ISLAND, N. Y.

MY DEAR MR. KOHLSAAT: July 2nd, 1917.

Those are very interesting letters. I return them and I thank you for having let me see them. It was a great pleasure to have caught a glimpse of you the other day. Let me see you whenever you come to New York, and if possible come out to Oyster Bay for lunch or dinner.

Faithfully yours,

(Signed) THEODORE ROOSEVELT.

Mr. H. H. Kohlsaat,
1440 First Natl. Bank Bldg.,
Chicago, Ills.

We met several times during the following year, and on March 12 I received the following letter from him:

OYSTER BAY

LONG ISLAND, N. Y.

DEAR H. H.   March 12, 1918.

Three cheers for you! Now, when you next come to New York you must let me know and come out here to lunch or dinner. You can bet I am going to act just along the lines you advise in your letter!

Faithfully yours,

(Signed) THEODORE ROOSEVELT.

Mr. H. H. Kohlsaat,
1440 First National Bank Bldg.,
Chicago, Ill.

The last letter I received from the colonel was written October 17, 1918. The lines he wrote in

THE KANSAS CITY STAR

OFFICE OF
THEODORE ROOSEVELT

NEW YORK OFFICE
347 MADISON AVENUE

October 17, 1918.

Dear H. H.

I do wish good folks like Victor
Lawson would take the trouble to read what I
have said. I have expressly stated again and
again that I was, and should be glad to see an
international league, but it must be as an
addition to and not as a substitute for our
own prepared strength. As a matter of ~~mere~~ *more truthfulness*
~~process~~ Lawson ought to use his great ability in pointing
out that at this moment we have a league in
connection with the allies and that when we *had* failed
to back up our allies by going to war with Turkey,
we are doing everything we can to establish a
precedent which would render any league of the
kind utterly worthless for the future. *President Wilson*

has done all everything Lawson in this edit Smith says
Staff he condemns; I have
not done them; why ask
he not — Faithfully yours,

Mr. H. H. Kohlsaat,
1440 First National Bank Bldg.,
Chicago, Ill.

Theodore Roosevelt

energetically attack Wilson!

with a pen show he was a very ill man even at that time. He died January 6, 1919:

THE KANSAS CITY "STAR"

Office of
Theodore Roosevelt

New York Office
347 Madison Avenue

October 17, 1918.

DEAR H. H.

I do wish good folks like Victor Lawson would take the trouble to read what I have said. I have expressly stated again and again that I was, and should be glad to see an international league, but it must be as an addition to and not as a substitute for our own prepared strength. As a matter of mere truthfulness Lawson ought to use his great ability in pointing out that at this moment we have a league in connection with the allies and that when we have failed to back up our allies by going to war with Turkey, we are doing everything we can to establish a precedent which would render any league of the kind utterly worthless for the future. President Wilson has done the very things Lawson in this editorial says that he condemns. I have *not* done them; why does he not energetically attack Wilson?

Faithfully yours,
(Signed) THEODORE ROOSEVELT.

XLI

PRESIDENT WILSON AND CABLE LINES

NOVEMBER 19, 1918, eight days after the armistice was signed, President Wilson decided to go to the Peace Conference in Paris, starting immediately after Congress met in December.

I was in Washington, Wednesday, November 20, when the morning papers announced the government would take over the cable lines. Postmaster-General Burleson already had the control of the land wires of the Western Union and Postal Companies; also the telephone-lines.

It was a shock to the country, especially to the press, to have the government take control of the cables after peace had been declared. It did not have the excuse even of being a war measure.

I called on Secretary of the Treasury McAdoo, and told him it was a mistake; that the press of the country, regardless of political bias, would think it was an attempt to control the news service from Paris; that Mr. Wilson's decision to go personally would emphasize that belief, and the President ought to reverse the Postmaster-General, who, of course, was acting under his orders. I said to Mr. McAdoo: " You will suffer along with the President." He answered: "Don't jump on me; I knew nothing about it until I saw it in the morning papers." I asked if it was possible the President would take such an important step without consulting his cabinet. McAdoo said he did not believe any member of the cabinet, with the exception of the Postmaster-General, knew a thing about it. After some further conversation I asked him to see the President and try to persuade him to change the order. With considerable emphasis he hit the door-post and said: "By ——, I will to-night."

Returning to the hotel, I wrote the President, and made much the same argument as I had done to Mr. McAdoo, with as forceful words as I could put on paper. I thought he would resent my remarks, and never expected to hear from him again, but to my surprise he wrote me the following letter two days later:

THE WHITE HOUSE
WASHINGTON

22 November, 1918.

MY DEAR MR. KOHLSAAT:

I realize the force of what you say in your kind note of the twentieth about the cables, but it is absolutely necessary for their proper administration that they should be administered as a single system, and I have not the least fear that the misrepresentations you have in mind will do any harm. They are too contemptible to be worthy of notice, and it will presently become evident that what we did was done in the course of business. I am none the less obliged to you for your generous concern in the matter.

Cordially and sincerely yours,
(Signed) WOODROW WILSON.

Thursday, the 21st, I returned to New York. Friday evening my attention was called to a bulletin in the late edition of *The Evening Mail* stating Secretary of the Treasury McAdoo had resigned. While I was reading, La Roux, bell captain of the Biltmore, came to me and said: "There are Secretary Lansing and Mrs. Lansing standing near the elevator." I went to them and asked Mr. Lansing if he had seen the McAdoo resignation rumor. He said: "Yes, they telephoned it to my room from down-stairs. I rang up the Associated Press and confirmed it. What does it mean?" I asked him when he had left Washington. He said: "This morning, and nothing was known of it then." I then told him of my interview with Mr. McAdoo, Wednesday, and his promise to see President Wilson that night. Mr. Lansing said: "That's right; he did see the President Wednesday night. I rang up the White House, and was told that he was closeted with Mr. McAdoo, and had left orders not to be disturbed."

What took place between the President and Mr. McAdoo they alone know, but it seems strange Mr.

22 November, 1918.

My dear Mr. Kohlsaat:

I realize the force of what you say in your kind
note of the twentieth about the cables, but it is absolutely
necessary for their proper administration that they should
be administered as a single system, and I have not the least
fear that the misrepresentations you have in mind will do
any harm. They are too contemptible to be worthy of notice,
and it will presently become evident that what we did was done
in the course of business. I am none the less obliged to
you for your generous concern in the matter.

Cordially and sincerely yours,

Woodrow Wilson

Mr. H. H. Kohlsaat,
The New Willard, Washington, D.C.

McAdoo should suddenly resign just as the President was leaving for France. In an interview Mr. McAdoo said he was compelled to resign for financial reasons; that he could not live on his salary; but it is possible to believe he could have held on a few weeks longer. I have always thought he resented being ignored in such an important move as taking over the cable lines without consulting the cabinet. I have been more or less intimate with the Presidents for nearly forty years, and do not believe any other President so completely ignored his official family.

There has never been any explanation why the cables were taken, but I presume the "business" reasons Mr. Wilson wrote of in his letter of November 22 were prompted by Theodore Vail; Newcomb Carlton, president of the Western Union Telegraph Company; Senator Murray Crane; and their associates. Twenty-five years ago John W. Mackay, of the Postal Company, said to me in substance: "I want the government to handle the telegraph-lines to relieve us of the blackmailing States attorneys in the counties we pass through."

XLII

MR. WILSON AND THE LEAGUE OF NATIONS

I AM a strong believer in the League of Nations, and am sure Mr. Wilson's devotion to that great cause was and is sincere.

During the Peace Conference in Paris I did everything in my power to bring about the co-operation of this country with our Allies, and still believe we shall have to join in some such movement before Europe can get out of her ghastly situation.

Many cables and letters passed between Colonel House and myself. I will print only the two following:

COMMISSIONER PLENIPOTENTIARY OF THE UNITED STATES OF AMERICA

DEAR MR. KOHLSAAT: Paris, April 25, 1919.

Your letter of April 7th reaches me this morning and I want to write and let you know how much I appreciate both your cables and letters.

Of course we realize that the Covenant is not a perfect document, but no American who was on the ground while it was being formed, could fail to recognize the many and delicate problems we had to face and overcome in order to have a workable League.

Everything has been very tense here during the past

week on account of the Italian crisis. Orlando has now gone home in order to try to work out something with his Parliament. I am sorry for him as he is one of the finest characters in the Conference. I hope we may yet be able to come to some agreement.

I have definitely decided to remain in England during the summer in order to work out with Lord Robert Cecil and some others, questions relating to the organization of the League. The sooner we succeed in getting it in shape to function, the better it will be for the entire world.

We are hoping that matters will be ready to close here by the end of May. We expect to detach "specialists" from now on as they finish their particular subjects, and only retain those who are actually needed.

With warm regards and good wishes, I am,

Your sincere friend,

(Signed) E. M. HOUSE.

Hon. H. H. Kohlsaat,
The Chicago Club,
Chicago.

P. S. It has been a great comfort to both the President and me to feel that we had your sympathy and support.

COMMISSIONER PLENIPOTENTIARY OF THE UNITED STATES OF AMERICA

Paris, June 26, 1919.

MY DEAR FRIEND:

Your letter of June 9th comes this morning. You can never know what a comfort your friendship has been during these trying months. In my opinion, no one has done more to further the cause of the League of Nations than you. Your influence is so great, and your suggestions are so practical that you have accomplished more than seemed possible.

I am leaving for London in a few days, and in the future please address me in care of the American Embassy there.

I shall miss our dear Lady Paget. Of course, you know that she died here some weeks ago.

The articles you send from *The Times*, *The New Republic* and *The Tribune* are illuminating. I have read them with the greatest interest and will pass them on to the President.

With all good wishes, I am,

Sincerely your friend,

(Signed) E. M. HOUSE.

H. H. Kohlsaat, Esq.
Chicago Club,
Chicago, Ill.

P. S. Since dictating this I have your letter enclosing the plan of the Princess Cantacuzène which I shall bring before those who are working on the Russian problem. Of course, matters have moved considerably since she wrote and doubtless to her satisfaction. I am also writing to her.

President Wilson left Paris at the end of June, 1919. After his arrival in Washington I saw him three times during July and August. During my first visit, July 10, he dictated the following: "The President is open-minded as to every proposition of reasonable interpretation, but will not consent to any proposition that we scuttle."

To maintain privacy, the President suggested I address the outside envelope to Mrs. Wilson, and enclose my letter in another envelope addressed to him.

On my second visit, about July 25, he came into

the Blue Room at 9.30 in the morning looking very ill. He was weak and trembling. I said: "You are too ill to take that long trip to the Pacific coast. The heat will be intense in Ohio, Indiana, Illinois, Iowa, and Nebraska. You will break down before you reach the Rockies." With his voice full of emotion he said: "I don't care if I die the next minute after the Treaty is ratified."

The President indulged in no heroics. We were alone. He meant it.

I suggested he postpone his trip three weeks and send for the Republican senators one at a time. He did so. After he had seen a dozen or more, the threatened railroad strike took all his time and strength.

I saw him again August 17, and urged him to accept the Lodge reservations. He promised to send me a memorandum of just what changes he would stand for. I returned to New York, and received the following letter on the 19th:

THE WHITE HOUSE
WASHINGTON
18 August, 1919.

My dear Kohlsaat,

I have not sent you the memo. we spoke of because immediately after I saw you I learned of the wish of the Senate Committee to come to the White House for an interview (a public interview), and it at once occurred to me that the best use I could make of the occasion would be to make my whole position as clear as possible, and I knew no exposition I could send you could reach you in time to be serviceable. I hope that the conference tomorrow will clear the air, in a sober and wholesome way. If it does not, other ways must be found. The editorial in yesterday's issue was a "cracker jack."

Cordially and sincerely yours,
(Signed) WOODROW WILSON.

P. S. This is my own handwriting, though it may not look like it!

W. W.

A few days later Mr. Wilson started on his trip to the coast, and came home a wreck, September 29.

October 20 I wrote the President again, strongly urging him to accept the Lodge reservations rather than have the Treaty rejected entirely, enclosing my letter in an envelope addressed to Mrs. Wilson. On the 25th I received the following note from Mrs. Wilson:

THE WHITE HOUSE

WASHINGTON

Oct. 23, 1919.

MY DEAR MR. KOHLSAAT:

I am returning herewith your note addressed to the President. As the doctors insist nothing be brought to him which is not absolutely essential and not knowing the purport of your message I think you will appreciate the wisdom of their precaution.

Cordially yours,
(Signed) EDITH BOLLING WILSON.
(Mrs. Woodrow Wilson.)

18 August, 1919.

THE WHITE HOUSE
WASHINGTON.

My dear Kohlsaat,

I have not sent you the memo. we
spoke of because immediately after I saw
you I learned of the wish of the Senate
Committee to come to the White House for
an interview (a public interview), and it
at once occurred to me that the best use
I could make of the occasion would be to
make my whole position as clear as possible, and I knew no exposition I could send
you could reach you in time to be serviceable. I hope that the conference to-morrow
will clear the air, in a sober and wholesome way. If it does not, other ways must
be found. The editorial in yesterday's
issue was a "cracker jack".

Cordially and sincerely Yours,

Woodrow Wilson

This is my own handwriting, though it may
not look like it!

W. W

XLIII

THE BREAK BETWEEN PRESIDENT WILSON AND COLONEL HOUSE

THE question has been asked many times: "What caused the break between President Wilson and Colonel House?" I recall that an admirer of President Wilson's career and policies was asked this question. He replied: "I believe Mr. Wilson is constitutionally incapable of sustaining a lasting friendship."

It is probable Mr. Robert Bridges, of Charles Scribner's Sons, and Mr. Cleveland H. Dodge, both of New York, will contest this view; but whether correct or not, it is my belief if Mr. Wilson had retained the friendship and followed the advice of Colonel House, he would have seen the "League of Nations" an accomplished fact, with over 90 per cent of the articles of the Treaty ratified by the United States Senate.

I know Colonel House intimately. We walk together nearly every day. We have one bond in common: neither of us ever had any political ambition or desire for office.

He has repeatedly told me he does not know why

President Wilson dropped him; neither verbally nor by the written word has he received any explanation for the change in their relations.

Under great pressure to grant interviews, he has refused to talk or write on the subject. No man ever deserved the title of "The Silent Man" more than he.

When Colonel House realized that President Wilson no longer sought his companionship or advice, it cut him to the heart; but no one ever heard him utter a word of complaint. He greets the humiliation of the newspaper gibes with a smile. He knows he gave Woodrow Wilson all it was his to give— loyal, whole-hearted, devoted support, with not one thought of self. He probably could have had any office in the gift of the President or his native State of Texas, but declined every honor.

Under the pen-name "Pollio" a writer in the New York *Times*, March 29, 1921, tells what he thinks caused the break. He says:

Mr. Lansing in his book "The Peace Negotiations" says with the exception of Colonel House the United States Peace Commissioners were ignored by President Wilson in Paris.

The reference to Colonel House brings up the frequently asked question on both sides of the Atlantic, "What was the cause of the break between President Wilson and Colonel House?" No answer to that question has ever been made, simply because there was no break. A close friend of both men says that there never was any disagreement, verbal or written, and that Colonel House is completely in the dark as to the reason of Mr. Wilson's change in his attitude toward him.

The friendship began in 1911 and continued until about the time Mr. Wilson started on his trip across the continent in August, 1919, to make his plea for the League of Nations.

Colonel House was asked to remain in France by Mr. Wilson to be on call for any emergency that might arise after the President left for the United States in the end of June.

The President returned to Washington from his Western trip, Sept. 29, completely broken down with a nervous collapse. On October 4 he had a stroke of paralysis and was unconscious for nearly a week and semiconscious for over a month. His partial recovery was very slow and for three months he saw no one but Mrs. Wilson, his doctors and his nurses. During that period all state papers were given to Mrs. Wilson first. If she was in doubt as to the possible effect that they would have on the President she submitted them to Dr. Grayson. If he thought that Mr. Wilson was strong enough to pass judgment on them without excitement, they were shown to him. If not, they were passed upon by Secretary of the Treasury Houston and one or two others in whom she had confidence.

When the President returned to Washington, a very sick man, and it was uncertain when he could again take up the duties of his office, Colonel House, who had been advised by surgeons in Paris to have an operation, decided to come home with Mrs. House. About the end of October he returned to New York, a very sick man.

For the next few weeks he had no communication whatever with the President, which fact was made a subject of much unpleasant comment and conjecture in the newspapers.

Since then there has been but little correspondence between the two, and none of the old relationship.

The only possible explanation of the cause of the severance is one of deduction which the reader can draw for himself.

Mr. Wilson was an enigma to the European statesmen. His position was so powerful they wanted his help and influence, but did not know how to approach him. He does not encourage intimacy. As one of his greatest admirers, a well-known American, said: "I have known the President for many years and have great respect and admiration for him, but I would as soon think of striking him in the face as to slap him on the back or put my arm around his shoulder."

During the tense days of the Peace Conference President Wilson, Lloyd George, Clemenceau and Orlando, the so-called "Big Four," met nearly every day. Frequently Clemenceau would call on Colonel House, an old friend, and discuss the questions that were likely to arise. Premier Orlando and Lord Robert Cecil, representing Lloyd George, also an old friend, were constantly in conference with the Colonel, as were the Premiers, delegates and public men from every country represented in Paris.

Percy Hammond, correspondent for the Chicago *Tribune* at the Peace Conference, wrote:

Mr. Wilson was visiting Colonel House when the British Premier's card came up. The Colonel graciously excused by the President, returned soon after and resumed the conversation. A few minutes later M. Clemenceau asked for a private interview, and again Colonel

House bowed himself out with apologies. He had been back but a short time when Signor Orlando was announced, requesting a moment's conference. Mr. Wilson once more waited, and on Colonel House rejoining him showed nothing of annoyance at the contretemps, but according to the casual historian of the Crillon, the incident darkened the landscape of a great friendship and the President and the Texan were intimate no more.

XLIV

REPUBLICAN NATIONAL CONVENTION
OF 1920

THE last Republican national convention met in Chicago, June 8, 1920. It was a headless affair. A Mark Hanna was needed to guide the chaotic mass of delegates, most of them in a national convention for the first time.

The awful heat, the steaming crowds, and the strike of hotel waiters made life almost unendurable for those poor mortals compelled to live in hotels and committee rooms. There was very little sleep for any one.

General Leonard Wood and Governor Frank O. Lowden, of Illinois, were the leading candidates. Friday afternoon and Saturday forenoon it looked as if Governor Lowden would be the nominee. He had proved himself to be a great executive. When he took office he found a little over $500 in the treasury and a lot of unpaid bills. At the end of his term, four years later, the State was free of debt and had a couple of million dollars in the treasury. Illinois at that time—1920—was a State to emulate.

Governor Lowden's fame had gone over the country. It was a period that needed a business adminis-

you accept for a full term of service the extremely important office which you have so aptly suggested. I have no doubt it is highly important and extremely valuable to have a brutal friend. I am sure it is exceedingly important to have some source of unfailing truth. If you will assume that responsibility you will be rendering both me and the country a very great service. I am always glad to hear from you and I would be glad to sit down now and chat with you for a half hour or more to get your view on pending problems. I had thought to ask you to do me that favor, but have been thinking perhaps you were going to take a run to the Southland and that I might more conveniently to both you and me see you in Florida during the early part of February. Pray, do not wait to have me send for you. When you have anything I ought to know see that it gets to me either in person or otherwise.

I am complying with your request respecting the return of Colonel Roosevelt's letter.

With very kindest regards, I am,
Very truly yours,
WGH–EBU (Signed) WARREN G. HARDING.

The letter from Colonel Roosevelt that Mr. Harding refers to was the following from Cairo, Egypt, as he came down the Nile from his African trip:

Cairo, March 27, 1910

DEAR MR. KOHLSAAT:

I have already told the Hamilton Club that if I speak in Chicago it will be to them, that is if I speak within the next six or eight months. So I cannot accept the Commercial Club's very kind invitation. I was greatly pleased with your editorial the other day in which you referred to Roosevelt's brutal friend!

Faithfully yours,
(Signed) THEODORE ROOSEVELT.

H. H. Kohlsaat, Esq.,
The Chicago *Record-Herald*.

President Harding has given me little opportunity to function as "brutal friend." My only criticism has been his appointment of Colonel Harvey as ambassador to England, and I am ready to modify that criticism, as reports from London, through the press and returning travellers, indicate that Colonel Harvey has overcome some of his faults, and has gained the respect and personal regard of our English friends, and also Americans who formerly were his strongest critics.

In October, 1922, Mrs. Harding was stricken with an almost fatal illness. Leading physicians and surgeons had been summoned to the White House. Bulletins were issued at intervals and the whole country was stirred with sympathy for the wife of the President, who, in eighteen months, had endeared herself to the people. She had taken deep interest in throwing the White House open to the public. Thousands passed through the historic rooms every day. She gave many brilliant social functions attended by diplomats and society people of Washington, and also lawn parties for wounded

From a photograph, copyright Baker Art Gallery

PRESIDENT HARDING

soldiers and sailors, and Easter egg-rolling parties
for the children. When the doctors' bulletins were
made public, they greatly alarmed the country.
Prayers were offered in nearly all the churches and
in public gatherings for her recovery. I attended a
luncheon in the Lawyers' Club in the Trinity Building. There were several hundred men present. A
gentleman arose and rapped for order and asked
the waiters to stand still in their places and then
said: "Gentlemen, I will ask you to stand for a
moment in silent prayer for the recovery of the wife
of our Chief Magistrate." The waiters stood with
their trays held high in the air and the members of
the club with their heads bent in silent prayer. It
was a sight I shall never forget. Mrs. Harding has
taken her place beside Mrs. Cleveland and Mrs.
Roosevelt as a White House hostess.

The Harding administration by the Conference
called for the Limitation of Armaments, November
11, 1921, I believe, will go down in history as having done more to advance the cause of peace in the
world than has been accomplished in 2,000 years.

I hope I do not violate a confidence when I tell
of a talk with the President in January, 1922, about
a week before the signing of the treaties by the
Powers gathered in Washington, and some two
months before they were ratified by the Senate.

We were sitting before the fireplace, where a few

sticks of wood blazed brightly. Resting his head wearily on his hand, gazing into the fire, the President said, in substance:

"The success or failure of this administration depends on the ratification or rejection of these treaties. Every administration's name in history rests on one or two acts. If these treaties are ratified by the Senate, then this administration's name is secure in history. If the treaties are defeated, nothing I can do the balance of my term can be of more than passing interest, which will be forgotten in a few years."

The reader can find no better theme for thought and discussion than to enumerate the great acts of our Presidents. Try it.

XLVI

A LETTER FROM LYMAN J. GAGE

In closing this series of Recollections I am taking the liberty of including a letter from Lyman J. Gage, Esq., now in his eighty-seventh year, who was Secretary of the Treasury in McKinley's cabinet in 1901, when McKinley was assassinated. He and Elihu Root, seventy-seven years old, Secretary of War, are the only members of that cabinet living.

Point Loma, California.
June 16th, 1922.

Mr. Herman H. Kohlsaat,
   Chicago, Ill.
My Dear Kohlsaat:—
   During the passing years, which have flown so swiftly, I have been frequently visited by returning thoughts of you. These thoughts of you were always bright and cheering, in their nature, containing in no degree whatever, as so frequently happens, any element of the disagreeable.

   No! the current of friendly sentiment has flowed steadily on uninterrupted by back wash or disturbing rapids, and I have carried the hope that reciprocally the former days with their memories of our friendly intimacy, possess an undiminished value of their own to you. With me they are endearing pictures which brighten my days.

   It isn't much the fashion for men to indulge in sentimental expression to their fellow men, but age has its privileges and immunities, and into that group, we call the aged, I have come. You, yourself, will join that group, when time allows, and even now the disparity in years is hard to realize, since I feel assured the *hearts* of both of us still beat with the spontaneity of life's full vigor.

The foregoing is rather a long preface to what I am now impelled to write. Impelled I am at the moment by the reading of your articles in *The Saturday Evening Post.*

Speaking generally of these articles, they are charming by their naïve frankness and bring into vivid life the historical and political events of twenty-five years ago. Numbers of my friends have expressed their delight in the reading of them.

To some of them, it is a story of "long ago," but to me, it's as fresh as the happenings of yesterday. Of course, to me and mine, it has the added value of personal reference and I feel quite "set up" and revivified by your most kind and friendly narration as, in a modest way, I am involved therein. I see that Brother Lodge is not satisfied with your statement of memories concerning him. But as for me, why I'll stand by Kohlsaat—especially, since I don't like Lodge anyway.

I shall be looking for the articles yet to come with growing interest. Having had my "day in court," I shall be glad to be now dismissed from further notice, and pleasantly reflect that of me there will be no probability of "further mention."

I congratulate you on the quality of your presentation. It is a decided contribution to the gathered facts which go to make up history. I am glad you are doing it, and join my thanks to all the others you will deserve and no doubt will receive.

Not knowing your address at the moment, I am mailing this to Chicago, on the theory that you will get it in due course, wherever you may be.

Cordially yours,

(Signed) LYMAN J. GAGE.

INDEX